# DIVA
## The Courageous
## The Visionary
## The Fabulous

Edited by Kate Bailey

With contributions from Veronica Castro,
Sasha Geffen, Keith Lodwick, Lucy O'Brien,
Miranda Sawyer and Jacqueline Springer

V&A Publishing

First published by V&A Publishing to accompany the exhibition
*DIVA*, 24 June 2023 – 7 April 2024, Victoria and Albert Museum,
South Kensington, London SW7 2RL

© Victoria and Albert Museum, 2023

Distributed in North America by Abrams, an imprint of ABRAMS

The moral right of the authors has been asserted.

ISBN 9781 83851 035 0

10 9 8 7 6 5 4 3 2 1
2027 2026 2025 2024 2023

A catalogue record for this book is available from the British
Library.

Designer: Joe Ewart
Copyeditor: Johanna Stephenson
Indexer: Nic Nicholas
New photography by Sarah Duncan, V&A Photographic Studio
Printed in China by Toppan Leefung

**V&A Publishing**

Supporting the world's leading
museum of art and design,
the Victoria and Albert
Museum, London

Page 2
Screenprint of Marilyn Monroe by Andy
Warhol, 1967
V&A: CIRC.121-1968

Page 5
Rihanna, in an ensemble by Galliano, attends
the *Heavenly Bodies: Fashion & The Catholic
Imagination* exhibition gala at the Costume
Institute, The Metropolitan Museum of Art,
New York, 2018

Pages 6–7
Cover artwork for Björk's *Fossora* album, 2022.
Photograph by Viðar Logi; creative direction by
Björk and James Merry

Page 8
*The Clodion Venus*; tinted Parian ware, after
Clodion (Claude Michel) by Minton, 1873
V&A: 831-1873

Page 10 and cover
Grace Jones with flowers at the Drury Lane
Theatre, London, October 1981. Photograph by
David Corio

Page 11
Marlene Dietrich in a promotional shot for
*No Highway in the Sky* (directed by Henry
Koster), 1951. Photograph by Angus McBean
V&A: S.1581-2015

Page 192
Josephine Baker in top hat and tails for a
performance at the Prince Edward Theatre,
London, 1933. Photograph by Piaz Studios
V&A: 89/1716

# Director's Foreword

Carved onto the 1909 façade of the V&A's South Kensington building stands an imposing succession of full-size figures surveying the street below. This impressive company of craftsmen, artists and architects – a shop window celebrating British output – includes William Morris, John Constable, J.M.W. Turner, Thomas Chippendale and Josiah Wedgwood, to name a few. Inside, this heraldry of creativity continues in the museum's niches and friezes, including parts of the V&A's 'Valhalla' that honour European masters of art and design – from Donatello to Da Vinci – through a series of life-size gold mosaic portraits.

However, women artists and female voices are notably absent. While today the V&A is an institution that champions creativity in all its forms – in recent years spotlighting artists, designers and photographers such as Frida Kahlo, Julia Margaret Cameron and Mary Quant – the first Victorian audiences to the museum were educated in art and design that had been created and curated by men.

Those audiences would have been familiar with an idea of the diva as a reflection of divine feminine power, as described by French critic Théophile Gautier in 1835. In the *DIVA* exhibition and its accompanying publication Gautier's ideal is examined and exploded, in a celebration of the diva as an empowered expression of identity in performance – across culture, race and gender. It considers how the muse became the diva, how the Victorian opera singer transformed into the twenty-first-century global megastar, and how the diva across history has played a role in driving social and political change. It addresses how the term 'diva' began to be deployed negatively, how this reflected changing perceptions of women and performance, and how the term has been reclaimed.

But at the heart of *Diva* is a celebration of exceptionally talented performers who have used their voice and art to inspire generations. Their powerful stories will be revealed through a showstopping display of creativity from across the V&A's collections, as well as global loans from artists and international institutions. From Jenny Lind to Maria Callas, Sarah Bernhardt to Lady Gaga, Josephine Baker to Beyoncé, Dolly Parton to Rihanna, Marlene Deitrich to Prince, *Diva* celebrates the fabulous, courageous, ingenious art of the performer.

We are enormously grateful to the artists, designers and practitioners who have contributed to the development of this exhibition. Their generosity provides a unique opportunity for V&A visitors to engage with their limitless creativity and vision. We would also like to express our gratitude to Kathryn Uhde for her support of the exhibition. Finally, thanks go to Lead Curator Kate Bailey, as well as Exhibition Research Assistant Veronica Castro, for bringing this contemporary Valhalla to its rightful place at the V&A.

*Tristram Hunt*

# Introduction: Redefining the Diva

Kate Bailey

Portrait of Adelina Patti by Franz Xaver
Winterhalter, oil on canvas, c.1865–70
Harewood House, Leeds

# The rise of the diva

**Once a virtuoso has been judged a diva, that is all that needs to be said, at least for the audience that gives her that epithet. The Diva becomes divine, she becomes the idol of the stage, the queen of the city, she is a siren, an enchantress, a charmer, someone who magnetizes her audience ... countless admirers, wildly applauded and acclaimed ... who is ultimately the object of a blind, passionate and unrivalled cult.[1]**

In the sixteenth century, as the female performer emerged from the all-male actor troupes, so did the diva. An Italian word commonly used since the fourteenth century to describe goddesses or deities, *diva* became a fitting description for exceptional female performers whose divine talents made them appear other-worldly.

Isabella Andreini (1562–1604) was an actor and musician whose astounding range and skill helped define the early diva. Described as a multifaceted genius, Andreini transcended her humble origins, was passionate about education and captivated audiences with her divine eloquence. Her motto, *Elevat Ardor* ('the flame rises'), reflects her sense of creative power. Her performances seemed to create a visceral experience that combined public intimacy and authenticity with a superhuman persona, attracting a cult of worshippers.[2]

By the eighteenth century the diva had found her place on stage and was recognized as a woman of exceptional artistic talent and power in Italian opera. Popular operas of the time were often based on classical mythology and featured gods and goddesses, and 'diva' was an epithet applied increasingly to the godlike heroine, the prima donna. As opera grew in popularity during the seventeenth and eighteenth centuries, the diva developed cult status. Contemporary poetry devoted to celebrating the prima donna provided a way for authors to express her artistic, physical and vocal presence. Poems and sonnets amplified the notion of the diva, drawing parallels between singers and goddesses and reflecting their power and command over their admirers. Significantly, the word specifically described female subjects on stage.

Giuditta Pasta as Norma in Bellini's *Norma*, pastel drawing by an unknown artist, c.1831
V&A: S.1692-2014

*Woman or rather, Diva, amidst the happy applause that resounds around you, you move the lips to smile and the eye to tears.*[3]

As early as 1826 the Parisian fashion magazine *Petit Courrier des Dames* described soprano Giuditta Pasta (1797–1865) performing in Rossini's *Semiramide* in December 1826 as 'La Diva, l'Adorata as they called her in Paris'.[4]

Opera as an art form spread across Europe during the nineteenth century and, as its popularity grew, the diva travelled too. There was a simultaneous shift in the balance of power in the opera house from the impresario and manager to the composer, as Italian composers such as Donizetti, Rossini and Bellini were creating and co-creating operas with powerful lead roles for the female soprano. These new operas combined extraordinary characters and music to accommodate the growing art, talent and ambition of the diva. Donizetti's *Lucia di Lammermoor* and Rossini's *Semiramide* were staged across the Continent, placing the tragic heroine centre stage and providing the singer with the lyrics and the melody to deliver vocal and emotional gymnastics. Thus bel canto ('beautiful singing') emerged as the quintessential singing style for the early divas.

One opera in particular had a significant impact in defining the diva in the nineteenth century: Bellini's bel canto opera *Norma*, which premiered in 1831 in Milan. The heroine is a high priestess whose character echoes Diana, the Roman goddess of woods and hunting. Norma performs the iconic aria 'Casta Diva' in a dramatic pagan ceremony, in which the sacred moon and the diva are immortalized as they are presented for worship. This highly charged visual narrative constructed around the voice of the prima donna established a diva aesthetic and concept. When this bel canto opera was first staged in Paris in 1835 with Italian singer Giulia Grisi (1811–1869) in the title role, it was to have a profound impact on audiences, including the French writer and critic Théophile Gautier:

*Giulia Grisi is Norma, and never, to be sure, did Irminsul have a more beautiful and more inspired high priestess. Song, passion and beauty, she has it all: bottled rage, sublime violence, threats and tears, love and anger. Never has a woman bared so much of her soul in the playing of a role...*

*The clouds part: a ray cuts through the dome of the forest, and the moonlight reveals the chaste whiteness in her face. It is then that Norma sings the beautiful aria beginning with the words 'Casta Diva' ... which seems imbued with the tender, melancholy soul of Bellini. To hear Grisi sing Casta Diva is one of the greatest pleasures one can imagine; the eye, the ear, and the soul are equally satisfied; in it the painter, the musician and the poet each find the ideal of their respective arts. Happy woman, thrice gifted...[5]*

Gautier's description was pivotal in the literary and bohemian discourse around the popularization of the diva concept in opera in France. He portrays the performance of the diva on stage as a total work of art – and recognizes the diva as thrice gifted, a perfect fusion of music, words and image. He goes on to establish links between generations of exceptional performers by referencing Spanish singer Maria Malibran (1808–1836) and further expresses the parallels between the live performer and classical antiquity:

*What secret excavation near the Parthenon produced that mask so pure, so classic, so vivacious, that the most violent emotion cannot distort, and which remains beautiful during the most dramatic agonies. Whenever she sings you know she has set herself after Malibran on the throne of gold, now left vacant and assumes her star, the diadem of the diva.[6]*

This male perspective, which imagines the performer as a marble statue, perhaps also reflects a fear of feminine creative and sexual power. While the diva remains celebratory and otherworldly in Gautier's writing, his definition denies the female performer mastery over her own artistry by considering her talent to be divinely bestowed. Thus Gautier magnified the artistic and aesthetic concept of the diva but detached the performer from reality, stripping her of power and agency.

With his radical enthusiasm for art for art's sake, Gautier harnessed the late nineteenth-century fascination with the diva in Paris at a time when women were often objectified by men, and when a prima donna, far from being respected by society, was often seen in the same light as a prostitute. These ideas were reinforced by French poet Charles Baudelaire in his *Painter of Modern Life*, in which men are represented as *flâneurs* and dandies and fashionable women as objects for male consumption.[7]

Hand-coloured print of Maria Malibran showing the singer in the role of Desdemona in a production of Rossini's *Otello*, Henri Decaisne, c.1830
V&A: S.3755-2013

Decaisne, del.t

MADAME MALIBRAN DE BERIOT.

(as Desdemona)

London Published by J. McCormick, 147, Strand.
Printed by Lefevre & Kohler, Newman St.

# Reinventing the diva

*Jenny Lind*, engraving by W. Roffe after a
drawing by A. Roffe, 1888
V&A: S.3415-2013

Left:
Papier maché box by Jennens & Bettridge
with mother of pearl inlay and painted
scenes, presented to Jenny Lind after a
charity concert in aid of the Queen's College
Hospital, Birmingham, 28 December 1848
V&A: S.276-1987

It is against this patriarchal backdrop that the nineteenth-century creative diva had to operate. As the century progressed, she had to negotiate a rapidly changing world, where image, technology and the demand for women's rights played a role in shifting perceptions of the performer both on stage and in society.

Before recorded sound, the diva was defined through a variety of media. On stage, pyrotechnic visual effects were often used to amplify her operatic performance, accentuating her complex character and tragic narratives. With the invention of new stage lighting techniques, by the middle of the nineteenth century she was literally placed in the limelight; towards the end of the century she was illuminated by electric light as opera houses used arclight to create spectacle and atmosphere.[8] Off stage, the diva was captured countless times in photography. This new, experimental art form disseminated her image, ensuring presence, relevance and familiarity to her admirers and initiating a cult of celebrity (p. 22).

Victorian London was an established home for Italian opera and an important stage for international stars. The city became central to the creation of the performer's image, with media and photographers constructing and sharing diva personas, magnifying their appeal and encouraging public interest in the stage goddesses through print and the popular cartes-de-visite. Publications such as the *Illustrated London News* were important publicity vehicles for the diva that reached upper- and middle-class audiences (p. 21). It seemed that Victorian society felt a need to separate the dramatic persona of the artist from the performer herself in a quest for respectability. Stories, reviews and profiles generated by the Victorian patriarchy projected a softened image of the diva's personality, often in marked contrast to her actual character and creativity. There appeared to be a fear of the alluring and dangerous power of the female voice, as many Victorians regarded women who pursued careers on the stage, as 'independent, defiant, seductive ... renegade, marginally feminine, de-classed'.[9] The idealization of the diva was a factor of the media's desire to uphold Victorian values, presenting the prima donna as a respectable woman – good, feminine and socially worthy.

Swedish opera singer Jenny Lind (1820–1887) was frequently depicted as the epitome of femininity,

Adelina Patti performing at the Albert Hall,
painted illustration in grisaille, probably
created for the *Illustrated London News*, 1901
V&A: S.390-2011

Left:
Costume worn by Adelina Patti in an
unidentified production, designed by
Morin-Blossier, c.1880s
V&A: S.478-1984

mythologized as an artist and a lady, a model of piety,
domesticity and purity. This idea reflected Lind's generous
spirit but also reinforced Gautier's classical obsession,
with contemporary visual artists capturing her female
beauty as an idealized Grecian or sculptural form (p. 19).
This widely produced imagery of the diva, stripped back
and simplified, also reinforced the Victorian notion that
good taste should be understated: 'Good taste forbids
too lavish a display of ornament'[10] – in marked contrast
to the flamboyance and exuberance displayed by future
generations of divas in control of their own image.

In 1883, when the *Oxford English Dictionary* first
defined the diva as 'a distinguished female singer, a prima
donna', Adelina Patti (1843–1919) was in her prime. This
Spanish-born Italian opera singer had travelled across North
and South America and was revered throughout Europe
as a goddess on stage. Her fame, success and wealth gave
her independence, status and freedom, unparalleled at
the time by any other profession available to women. To
Victorian audiences she must have seemed otherworldly
and her life unattainable.

At the height of her fame Patti was revered by admirers
worldwide, painted by the leading artists of the day (p. 12)
and second only to Queen Victoria as the most recognized
woman in Britain. She was not only able to finance the
purchase of her own castle, Craig-y-Nos in Wales, but in
1891 she added her own theatre to the site, based on
La Scala in Milan. Patti was an astute businesswoman
whose extravagant lifestyle was reflected in her choice of
fashionable dress. A stage costume designed for her by
Morin-Blossier – a leading Parisian fashion house founded
by Victoire Morin and Marie Blossier, renowned for
supplying gowns to European royalty[11] – demonstrates how
Patti's financial independence allowed her the creative
agency to style her own look. The Victorian diva had
reached 'royal' status.

The abundance of images of the diva, from cartes-de-
visite to engravings, were pivotal to Patti's public image.
They revealed star quality and respectability, further
amplified by narratives in print that projected the diva
as an idealized woman and role model who assumed
a philanthropic role in society. As a result, the Victorian
public perception of the opera diva was largely positive,
although confined within the expectations of a patriarchal

Adelina Patti as Aida, photograph, c.1895
V&A: S.138:307-2007. Guy Little Collection

society, muting, to some degree, her individuality and self-expression.

In the first decade of the new century the media continued to construct an image of Adelina Patti as powerful yet often demanding, creating a public fascination with diva behaviour and status, from beauty routines to contracts. On her US tour the *Los Angeles Times* stated that 'the diva was paid $5000 to sing two songs, and received a large allowance for herself and a private car for her own exclusive use';[12] on another occasion, when invited to sing outside her stage performance, 'the Diva showed no inclination to oblige'.[13]

Towards the end of the nineteenth century the Victorian stars of the stage, the divas of the spoken word, played an important role in shifting the cult of the diva, as the female performer found her voice and greater individuality and artistic freedom through drama. British actors Ellen Terry (1847–1928) and Vesta Tilley (1864–1952), French actor Sarah Bernhardt (1844–1923) and Italian star Eleanora Duse (1858–1924) created diverse and distinct roles both on stage and in society at large.

Sarah Bernhardt was renowned for her melodrama, using extravagant gesture to express emotion, particularly to express female suffering on stage.[14] Like the opera divas who performed tragic heroines, she could communicate intense emotion through her dramatic interpretation of strong characters. Throughout her long career Bernhardt also challenged gender boundaries and took on powerful stage roles both male and female, from Hamlet to Joan of Arc; her artistic excellence was recognized throughout Europe and across the Atlantic. As an exceptional, international and often eccentric star, she was depicted through a multiplicity of images, reflecting and encouraging the public's burgeoning fascination.

Czech Art Nouveau artist Alphonse Mucha created many of the 'divine images' of Bernhardt that boosted her fame and immortalized the image of the performer. Theirs was a mutually beneficial and creative collaboration: Bernhardt was both a muse for Mucha's distinctive artistic style and gave him the opportunity to design the posters advertising her US tours. Hugely popular with international audiences, the actor was in control of her own image and as early as 1912 presented a series of 'cinematograph films' in a private exhibition which revealed 'the diva' in 'various

Sarah Bernhardt as Joan of Arc, poster by
Eugène Grasset, 1890
V&A: E.190-1921

amusements and occupations'.[15] Bernhardt's popularity and ability to embrace new technology was seized on by the pioneers of early film as the stage goddess went on to inspire the next generation of cinema's heroines. The profound impact of Bernhardt's fame was reflected in dramatic newspaper headlines announcing her death.

Eleanora Duse, a rival of Bernhardt, adopted a different approach to achieve diva status. In contrast to Bernhardt's use of dramatic gesture, Duse was praised for her naturalism and the interiority and intimacy of her art, which was described as conveying an intelligence of performance with a more subtle presence. Duse's diva persona was more human and understated – indeed, she was notorious for not wearing make-up either on or off the stage (p. 25).[16]

Often described as more than an actor, theatrical trailblazer Ellen Terry was trained to perfection in the works of Shakespeare. Larger than life and with an international reputation, Terry was described by her son as more than an actress: 'She spread herself out and encompassed the stage, the stalls, the pit, gallery and somehow the air'.[17] Performing traditional roles, she appealed to respectable Victorian theatregoers and inspired a devoted following. Adoring fans remained fascinated by her performances; indeed, her interpretation of Lady Macbeth at the Lyceum in 1888 had the media speculating on the length of her hair thirty years after her original iconic performance, in a glimpse of the future tabloid press generating stories about the diva.[18] In her unconventional personal life Terry exploded traditional ideas of the Victorian woman, striving for independence and freedom. Having first been married to artist George Frederic Watts and then to architect Edward William Godwin, when her third marriage failed, to actor Charles Kelly, she 'gave him three quarters of what I earned and prayed him to go...'.[19]

At her retirement concert Terry performed on stage with Vesta Tilley, a music hall artist whose cross-dressing stage acts challenged notions of what a female performer could do. Together they provided a celebration of diva power across gender and identity, Terry providing feminine gravitas with Tilley, in military uniform, balancing this with a trim masculinity (overleaf). Her traditionally masculine style was embraced in the 1920s and '30s by film star Marlene Dietrich (1901–1992), who confronted conventional ideas of femininity by wearing trousers on and off the set.

Vesta Tilley on stage with Ellen Terry in the
final performance of her 'Farewell Tour',
1920

Eleonora Duse, pastel drawing by Rosina
Matovani Gutti, early 20th century
V&A: S.533-2018

# MISS ELLEN TERRY'S JUBILEE: THE GREAT ACTRESS IN FAMOUS RÔLES.

AS PORTIA IN "THE MERCHANT OF VENICE."
AT THE LYCEUM THEATRE.

AS LUCY ASHTON IN "RAVENSWOOD," WITH
SIR HENRY IRVING AT THE LYCEUM.

*Copyright Photo. by Leonard Craske.*

MISS ELLEN TERRY AND HER DAUGHTER,
MISS AILSA CRAIG, IN "THE GOOD HOPE."

A RECENT
PORTRAIT
OF
MISS
ELLEN
TERRY.

*Photo.
Lallie Charles.*

Terriss.                                 Irving.

AS QUEEN KATHERINE IN "HENRY VIII." WITH
IRVING AND TERRISS AT THE LYCEUM.

*Photo. Window and Grove.*

AS GUINEVERE IN "KING ARTHUR."

*Photo. Window and Grove.*

AS QUEEN KATHERINE IN "HENRY VIII."

On April 28 Miss Ellen Terry celebrates her jubilee on the stage. She first appeared as Mamillius in "The Winter's Tale" with Charles Kean at the Princess's Theatre. On that occasion she played before the Queen and Prince Albert. On the 28th Miss Ellen Terry appears at the Court Theatre and at the Adelphi.

Sheet music for 'You Can't Stop A Girl
From Thinking!' sung by Marie Lloyd and
composed by Tabrar, Harrington and
Le Brunn, 1897
V&A: S.75-1989

Left:
Page from the *Illustrated London News*
celebrating 'Miss Ellen Terry's Jubilee: the
great actress in famous roles', 28 April 1906
V&A: 38041021503354

Outside the Victorian theatre, in the music halls around Britain, female performers from the working classes were gaining recognition. Marie Lloyd (1870–1922), the most recognized British music-hall star, took advantage of her popularity and public profile when she supported the 1907 music hall strike. Demonstrating her social consciousness and activism, she asserted that 'we [the stars] can dictate our own terms. We are fighting not for ourselves but for the poorer members of the profession'.[20] In contrast to the international, multilingual diva of the opera stage, Lloyd's comic public persona gave an authentic voice to the working classes. Her art was not otherworldly, as the early ideal divas were expected to be, but as a celebrated female performer holding sway over a substantial audience, she holds her place in the diva pantheon. Lloyd had to navigate and perform within the overt misogyny and sexism of the music halls. Like Patti, she was self-sufficient through her earnings and gave a voice to a generation of women who wanted the new century to bring new rights and freedoms, a sentiment echoed in her musical monologue 'You Can't Stop a Girl from Thinking!'

Despite her professional success, Lloyd's own life was far from liberated and she struggled with difficult personal relationships. As with other divas who came before and after, a powerful professional life was no guarantee of personal contentment and often attracted public scrutiny, with tragic consequences.

As the nineteenth century drew to a close, and as women's voices became more empowered, the female performer redefined roles in new artistic spaces and challenged perceptions of what a diva could be beyond theatre and opera. This can be seen in the context of the European artistic fascination with the biblical figure of Salome. Following the first performance of the play by Oscar Wilde in 1896, there was a plethora of interpretations of this complex female protagonist. Salome's power as an exotic temptress and murderer was celebrated and feared by male composers and stage directors such as Richard Strauss and Max Reinhardt, and concurrently provided a powerful feminist vehicle for expression for a generation of female dancers. As the respectable opera diva was only permitted to sing the role of Salome in Strauss's opera, dancers, deemed at the time to have less status than singers, were invited to perform 'The Dance of the Seven Veils'.[21]

Beyond opera, dancers were eventually able to take on the role of Salome with greater agency and autonomy. In 1913 impresario Sergei Diaghilev commissioned a ballet production, *La Tragédie de Salomé*, as a vehicle for pioneering Russian prima ballerina Tamara Karsavina (1885–1978). Wearing a striking costume, she created an intoxicating performance that was risqué, bold and expressive. And visionary American performer Loie Fuller (1862–1928) enthralled audiences at the Comédie Parisienne with her sensual, fluid, interpretation of Salome that would electrify the dancing diva into the new realms of the moving image. Both artists captured the zeitgeist of Salome and used the character as a vehicle for their own creative modernity.

In 1904 Isadora Duncan (1877–1927), pioneer of modern dance, expressed her desire to empower women through their creativity, learning and self-expression. Her ambition was to establish a dance school that 'would not be a school of dance but a school of life…'.[22] Recognizing the power of her position as a potential influencer of young women and society, she outlined her mission, to create

> *a theatre where a hundred little girls shall be trained in my art, which they in their turn will better. In this school I shall not teach the children to imitate my movements, but to make their own. I shall not force them to study … I shall help them to develop those movements which are natural to them.*[23]

Duncan's statements ooze confidence and reflect her strong sense of self and sexuality. Her choice of fashion, such as classically inspired Fortuny gowns (overleaf) allowed freedom of movement, in marked contrast to the restrictive corsets of Victorian fashion. She asserted that the 'free modern woman would be more beautiful and more glorious than all women of past centuries…'.[24]

Like many performers, Duncan was aware of her own place in the history of the female performer. Indeed, she famously danced a tribute to Bernhardt on the night of her death.[25] Such intergenerational relationships are a consistent thread, as performers reflect on the achievements of their forebears while being acutely aware of their own legacies.

Tamara Karsavina in the role of Salome in Serge Diaghilev's ballet *La Tragédie de Salomé*, Ballets Russes, 1913. Photograph by Gerschel

Right:
Costume worn by Tamara Karsavina as Salome in Serge Diaghilev's ballet *La Tragédie de Salomé*, Ballets Russes, designed by Serge Sudeikine and made by Mme Ivaschenko of Caffi, St Petersburg, 1913
V&A: PROV.668-2022

'Delphos' dress designed by Henriette
Nigrin, possibly with Mariano Fortuny, for
Fortuny, pleated silk trimmed with amber
beads, Venice, 1920–3
V&A: T.22-1985

Postcard of Lyda Borelli, 1911. Photograph by
Emilio Sommariva

PAUL
COLIN

# Power struggles

**There is nothing connected with making a film that a woman cannot do as easily as a man.**[26]

Ellen Terry, Sarah Bernhardt and Marie Lloyd were divas driving the first wave of feminism from their positions of success on the stage. They needed creativity, ambition, resilience and attitude to succeed. In 1918, 8.4 million women in Britain over the age of 30 were allowed to vote for the first time. Performers overseas such as Josephine Baker (1906–1975) would have been galvanized by this development and inspired to fight similar battles for women's equality internationally. Singer, dancer and actor, Baker would become one of the great artists and role models for the next century – combining art, performance and politics both locally and internationally.

> I never took the easy path, always the rough one. But, you know when I took the rough path, I wanted to make it a little easier for those who followed me.[27]

Born in the USA, Baker performed in Black vaudeville theatre on Broadway before arriving in Paris in the 1920s. Here she adapted her American stage skills and developed a unique stage persona in the French music hall, constructing a distinct image and identity. Through her theatrical performances and the evolution of her iconic 'banana skirt', Baker reinvented herself and harnessed the contemporary audience's racialized fascination with 'exoticism' and non-Western culture.[28] Baker confronted and redefined highly offensive stereotypes and captivated audiences through her social, political and sexual power. Her popularity was strengthened by a world tour in 1928–9 and her performance in the stage show *Ziegfeld Follies* on her return to the US in 1936, which provided her with a voice on the international stage. She continued to fight against the societal weaponization of race and gender, and became a champion of a free and open society, combating

Plate from *Le tumulte noir* by Paul Colin depicting Baker and her famous 'banana skirt', 1929
V&A: NAL 38041800162273

the forces of racism and hypocrisy. As an ambassador for tolerance, Baker showed the world that song and dance could be not merely performance, but a political statement.[29] Her utopian dreams continued throughout her career: she became a spy for the French Resistance and mother to an international family – which she called her 'rainbow tribe' – adopting eight children to live with her at her castle in the Dordogne, Château des Milandes.

Baker defied and manipulated the objectification and sexualization of the male gaze in dance, successfully harnessing her image, popularity and power to support her own causes and political campaigns. As a political diva she provided a crucial voice in the fight for racial equality, alongside other American singers from across musical genres – opera, jazz, gospel, blues and soul – who used the power of their voices as a vehicle for protest, disruption and change. Artists like Billie Holiday, Aretha Franklin and Nina Simone, with their exceptional voices, ensured that the song of the modern diva became the message and that they as performers were powerful agents for change. The protest songs of the divas fighting against systems of oppression[30] would provide a foundation for future generations of fearless diva activists who continue to fight for change in society, but the mighty struggles faced by women of colour were different and complex as they also had to contend with racism and battle with discrimination (see Springer, pp. 82–103). Their fearless struggles for freedom were reinforced decades later in the powerful words of author, intersectional feminist and civil rights activist Audre Lorde, who wrote extensively about 'how racial difference creates a constant, if unspoken, distortion of vision'.[31] She stated: 'I am not free while any woman is unfree, even when her shackles are very different from my own'.[32]

As film became the most popular medium of mass entertainment in the new century, many of the opera, stage and dance divas were cast by silent movie studios as leading ladies of the screen. This was to have a huge impact on the public perception of the diva, as the early film makers constructed films around the personality and star quality of the female performers, building on their fame and image. Both Bernhardt and Terry made silent films

Mary Pickford on the cover of *The Ladies'
World,* April 1915

Left:
Theda Bara as the title role in *Cleopatra,*
Fox Film Corporation, 1917

before their retirement and when Josephine Baker starred in *La Sirène des tropiques* in 1927 she became the first woman of colour to star in a studio motion picture.

Lyda Borelli (1887–1959) was one of the first Italian actors to cross from theatre to film, securing her place as a diva of early cinema. Borelli portrayed intense characters who were doomed and otherworldly, often bordering on the supernatural, echoing the tragic heroines of opera (p. 31). Her visceral power was reflected in her immense popularity, with audiences attracted to her decadent, vampish persona: in *La fleur du mal*, for example, a film that echoes the symbolism of Baudelaire's nineteenth-century text, her performance was dark, highly charged and sexual.

Of course, in the silent movie – the spectacular visual and dramatic art form in which the diva was central – the diva's voice was itself silenced. Acclaimed soprano Geraldine Farrar (1882–1967) was seen but not heard in *Carmen* (1915), a silent adaption by Cecil B. DeMille of the opera by Georges Bizet. Although losing her voice did not stifle the extraordinary vitality and energy of this much-loved opera performer, early cinema audiences could no longer hear her. In the same year Carmen was also played by American actor Theda Bara (1885–1955) in a silent film directed by Raoul Walsh. Both stars created sensational and sublime – yet silent – interpretations of the role, harnessing Carmen's exoticism and sexuality to project an image of the femme fatale that shifted representations of the female body. In doing so they, like Bernhardt and Borelli, demonstrated how the diva could have agency over their own image and sexuality on film, far from the classical ideal constructed for the Victorian opera diva. Performers like Farrar and Bara who relocated to Hollywood were pivotal in redefining the modern interdisciplinary diva as they made the transition from live stage performance into film.

Theda Bara was among Hollywood's first stars of the silver screen. In 1917 she was one of the first actors to portray Cleopatra on screen, originating the blueprint for an iconic diva role, taken on later by the likes of Elizabeth Taylor and Cher (see p. 72). As an artist working in the early film studios, Bara experimented with her look, working alongside a curator of Egyptology from the Metropolitan Museum of Art, to become the Egyptian queen. Bara was an originator of the vamp image and demonstrated how artists at the time could have creative agency, self-styling

Original Poster for *All About Eve* (directed
by Joseph L. Mankiewicz), 1950

Left:
Ida Lupino directing *The Trouble with
Angels*, 1966

their look, from make-up and wig to costume. Her success
earned Bara at the height of her career £41,000 a week
in today's money. But it was the studios that seized and
controlled the narrative. Seeing the popularity of Bara as
the first femme fatale, they cast her in more than forty films,
harnessing her exoticism and casting her as a temptress
and seducer. The studios were responsible for changing
her name and her back-story – Theda Bara the Egyptian
temptress was in fact born Theodosia Goodman, a child
of Jewish immigrants from Cincinnati. Like many early silent
movie stars, she never made a talkie and saw her popularity
diminish as American tastes and movie storylines changed.
Her revealing costumes were eventually censored by
the authorities in 1930 and her films were subsequently,
tragically, lost to the world.

But the commercial Hollywood studios had seen that
audiences were hungry for sensational news and that the
diva, under their control, could take on multiple identities
and be the trigger for stories that would lead to box office
sales. It was not just about her image or her voice: the diva
became a publicity machine, controlled and driven by the
film's promotors. With pin-ups, public appearances, studio
magazines and interviews providing glimpses into the diva's
private life behind the scenes, the cult of celebrity was by
this time firmly established.

Yet some artists were ultimately able to take back
control. Marketed by the studios as 'America's sweetheart',
Mary Pickford (1892–1979; p.35) became the innocent and
wholesome star for a new generation, performing roles
in silent movies such as *Little Annie Rooney* (1925) and
*Dorothy Vernon of Haddon Hall* (1924). Pickford gained
huge popularity and critical acclaim and was eventually
able to harness her success to gain power over the studios.
Defying the existing studio system, Pickford bravely set
up United Artists in 1919 with Douglas Fairbanks and
Charlie Chaplin. This production company laid important
foundations for female independent stardom in the 1930s
and helped professionalize the business of acting. As an
empowered diva, Pickford was able to use her business
acumen and shrewd understanding of contracts to change
perceptions and enhance the careers of future female
artists.[33]

This mission of speaking truth to power while fighting
for gender equality in business was continued by other

Poster for *The Philadelphia Story* (directed by George Cukor), 1940, starring Katharine Hepburn, Cary Grant and James Stewart. Hepburn used her ownership of the film rights to the successful stage play to forge a Hollywood comeback.

Illustration of Clara Bow in a poster for *IT* (directed by Clarence G. Badger and Josef von Sternberg), 1927

Mae West poster designed by Alan Fletcher
of Pentagram, screenprint, 1988
V&A: E.408-2003

Right:
Mae West as Tira in *I'm No Angel* (directed
by Wesley Ruggles; screenplay by Mae
West), 1933

performers in the industry, including Clara Bow (1905–1965),
Katharine Hepburn (1907–2003) and Ida Lupino (1918–1995).
Clara Bow, 'it girl' flapper from Brooklyn, negotiated a
percentage-deal bonus that steered her from rags to riches.
Having arrived in Hollywood from the UK at the age of 14,
Lupino negotiated deals to keep three films outside studio
agreement and found ways to expand her role behind the
camera, forming her own production company in 1949.

The clash between Bette Davis (1908–1989) and
Jack Warner, co-founder of Warner Bros. Studios, in 1936
is perhaps the highest-profile of these off-screen studio
battles (see p. 67). Davis said of her situation, 'I was told I
had no right fighting like a man. Jack Warner told me he'd
teach me a lesson',[34] revealing the stark inequality for
women at the time. A lawyer acting against Davis stated
that 'this is a rather naughty young lady. What she wants
is more money.'[35] Her struggles and treatment by the
patriarchy epitomize the challenges faced by female artists
at the time and reflected the widespread negative view of
feminine power: 'When a man gives his opinion, he's a man.
When a woman gives her opinion, she's a bitch.'[36]

This portrayal of the Hollywood stars as demanding
and difficult can also be seen in the gossip magazines and
newspapers on both sides of the Atlantic. In the London-
based *Daily Herald* in 1936, Spike Hughes's 'Talking about'
column describes an unnamed 'Hollywood diva who
before she can go on set to play a scene has to have violin
and guitar play mood music' and 'a man must come on
set and take the temperature'.[37] This reinforces a negative
impression of a diva's behaviour that might otherwise have
been interpreted as an artist dedicated to delivering an
exceptional performance.

The Golden Age of Hollywood in the 1930s and '40s
presented the diva in a variety of modern roles to a critical
mass of women in Europe and the USA, yet this period
saw a dip in gender parity, with women underrepresented
as actors, directors and producers. The real power of the
Hollywood diva dwindled as independent film makers of
the 1910s and '20s were replaced by big studios. Due to
her demands for equality, status and respect, a performer
like Davis was projected as difficult on and off screen in an
attempt to undermine her power and influence. In 1947
an article in the *Los Angeles Times* stated that the year
undoubtedly would be the most testing for the 'cinema

diva', as the entertainment critic Edwin Schallert was expecting to see an increase in roles and box office returns for male actors: 'During the war days women had the edge ... but the men held forth as top fighters in pre-war days'.[38]

The power of the Hollywood diva was regularly overshadowed by sexism in the industry as successful female artists went head-to-head with their male counterparts in their battle for equality. With the artist's increasing boldness and drive to rock the status quo came an increasingly negative depiction of the diva, as many female performers were forced to work within the power structures of the studio system. This negative attitude and control gathered momentum later in the twentieth century and endemic misogyny has taken generations to unravel, finally given traction and attention with the #metoo movement.

One of those who had been rocking the status quo of male-dominated Hollywood since the 1930s was Mae West (1893–1980). In words from her screenplay for *I'm No Angel* (1933), which reflect her own rebellious spirit, she reassured her followers that 'When I'm good, I'm very good, but when I'm bad, I'm better'. This mantra gave a voice to future generations prepared to take on the spirit of non-conformity and disruption.[39] Some two decades later Marilyn Monroe (1926–1962) echoed this sentiment as an artist striving for creative freedom and perfection:

> I guess people think that why I'm late is some kind of arrogance and I think it is the opposite of arrogance.... The main thing is, I do want to be prepared when I get there to give a good performance to the best of my ability.[40]

These strong-minded statements about their artistic struggles contributed to perceptions of the diva in the public imagination, often through the lens of a media that would revel in tracing the rise and fall of the most powerful global artists. Consumers were fascinated by their strong personalities and the duality and tension between their public and private lives. For the diva, fame, life and art were under constant scrutiny. In 1952 the *Daily Mirror* exploited the discovery of nude photos of Monroe months before advertisements promoting her new movie *Don't Bother to Knock* used explicitly sexualized images with the strapline 'every inch a woman, every inch an actress'.[41]

Costume designed by Orry-Kelly, worn by
Marilyn Monroe as Sugar 'Kane' Kowalczyk in
*Some Like it Hot*
V&A: S.1647-2015

Right:
Marilyn Monroe with Tony Curtis and Jack
Lemmon in *Some Like It Hot* (directed by Billy
Wilder), 1959

In 1959, at the height of her fame, Monroe, as Sugar 'Kane' Kowalczyk in *Some Like It Hot* sang 'I wanna be loved by you' and captivated audiences in a performance that was comic and heartbreaking in equal measure. Wearing a little black shimmy flapper-style dress, Monroe's emotionally bruised character drinks from her hip flask with her cross-dressed co-stars before she entertains and dazzles in a showstopping musical and dance performance, reflecting the duality of the life of the diva on and off stage. Monroe was aware of the power of worshipping fans and how they contributed to her success: in her last interview she allegedly said, 'if I am a star, the people made me a star. No studio, no person, but the people did'.[42]

Monroe also used her talent, fame and popularity as a positive force for others. She persuaded the owner of the exclusive Mocambo Club in West Hollywood to book her friend Ella Fitzgerald (1917–1996), at the time a rising jazz star who was battling against racism and prejudice. 'On the opening night Monroe sat in the front row and ensured that the audience was liberally sprinkled with celebrities including Judy Garland and Frank Sinatra',[43] using her celebrity status to create publicity for the African American artist and generating audiences for what was to be a sellout run. Thus Monroe as a fan and a friend demonstrated diva solidarity and power, providing the highly gifted Fitzgerald with a significant career opportunity.

Returning to the world of opera, the birthplace of the diva, Maria Callas (1923–1977; overleaf) is often described as the ultimate diva. Despite widespread fascination for her private life and the intrusive public gaze, Callas remained passionate and vocal about her role as an artist seeking perfection: 'I am not an angel and do not pretend to be. That is not one of my roles. But I am not a devil, either. I am a woman and a serious artist.'[44]

Through the visceral and emotional power of her voice and the bel canto roles she performed, Callas connected to the past. In the words of director Franco Zeffirelli,

*Maria identified with Bellini's Norma greatly. In a way it was her own story. Maria after all is a high priestess – the high priestess of her art. Yet at the same time she is the most fallible of women. Very human. As Norma, Maria created the maximum of what opera can be. In a lifetime, one can see many great things in the theatre but to see Maria Callas in Norma, what is there to compare it to?*[45]

As creative artists of the 1950s, Callas and Monroe represent a catalyst for the next generation. Their personal frustrations with the containment of their art and creativity chimed with the theories expounded by Betty Friedan in *The Feminine Mystique*. Published in 1963, the year after Marilyn Monroe's tragic death, Friedan addressed women's discontent with a society that limited their opportunities: her treatise challenged women to stop conforming to the conventional picture of femininity, and to enjoy being New Women with identities and lives of their own.[46] Friedan is often associated with initiating the 'second wave' of feminism, raising critical interest in issues such as workplace equality, birth control and abortion, women's education – and the power of female creativity. The final chapter of *The Feminine Mystique*, 'A New Life Plan for Women', proposed that women can achieve 'the freedom to lead and plan their own life'.[47]

NORMA
ACT I
MME MENEGHINI·CALLAS
COVENT GARDEN
1952

Alan Barlow

Folk singer and activist Joan Baez performs
at an anti-Vietnam war rally in Trafalgar
Square, London, May 1965

# The diva reclaimed

As if with Friedan's mantra in mind, a new generation of empowered divas appeared in the 1960s, building on the foundations laid by their forebears, occupying traditionally male spaces and changing the dynamic between the female performer and subsequent generations of worshippers. In the world of opera the original nineteenth-century definition of the diva continues to evolve as modern opera voices continuously redefine and reinterpret iconic roles in opera houses worldwide. The rarity and brilliance of the performer's voice gives her a timeless, universal appeal, attracting a dedicated fan base as audiences travel across continents to see her perform. Exceptional voices have enabled divas of opera to retain their otherworldly power as they continue to shape and create new roles with creativity, emotion, and passion. Among these seminal performances have been Joan Sutherland (1926–2010) as Lucia (1961), Leontyne Price as Aida (1966; previous page) and Jessye Norman (1945–2019) as Ariadne (1985) to name but a few.

Outside the world of opera, one of the most prolific and iconic Middle Eastern vocalists of all time is Fairuz (Nouhad Wadie' Haddad), known as 'The Soul of Lebanon'. Her musical career, which began in 1950, spans six decades. Widely recognized as the greatest living Arab diva, Fairuz has performed across the world, from the Damascus Opera House to the MGM Grand in Las Vegas, demonstrating that the global term 'diva' can cross cultures, genres and continents, and that an exceptional voice can enable the diva to command an international fanbase.

The diva has also negotiated her place in rock, pop and country. Dolly Parton, who rose to fame as a singer and songwriter, is an astute businesswoman, while Barbra Streisand became the ultimate interdisciplinary artist, pushing boundaries on stage, in her recordings and in film, both in front of and behind the camera. Both artists overcame obstacles to redefine perceptions of the diva, as popular music provided women with a new platform and new audiences. Aretha Franklin and Joan Baez gave the diva voice for change, while in the 1970s Cher, Tina Turner and others broke free from their partnerships to forge new identities and careers, working with visionary fashion designers such as Bob Mackie to construct iconic stage personas.

The transformation of the diva continued into the 1980s with highly creative artists such as Grace Jones and Madonna emerging to express their sexuality and constantly reinvent their public personas. Often drawing from performers of the past, rising star Madonna was hailed as the diva of music and dance.[48] The liberation and transformation of the diva continued apace with male performers Elton John, Freddie Mercury and Prince. They demonstrated how the concept of the diva is fluid and could be harnessed and channelled on and off stage to create experimental new spaces in which male stars could express femininity and be as showstopping as their female counterparts. Elton John (p. 60) recalled:

> I kept pushing the live show, trying to make it more over-the-top and outrageous – I started employing professional costume designers and egging them to do whatever they wanted, no matter how insane; more feathers, more sequins, brighter colours, bigger platforms.[49]

Meanwhile, Debbie Harry and Siouxsie Sioux established themselves as the archetypal pop-punk and goth divas respectively. As if to soundtrack it all, 'soul diva'[50] Aretha Franklin recorded 'sisters are doing it for themselves' with Annie Lennox, providing a cross-generational soundtrack for girl power.

In the 1990s and beyond, the diva has broken into newer musical genres, such as hip-hop and rap with Missy Elliott and Ms Lauryn Hill. These disruptive and empowered divas are trailblazers who use their voice, lyrics, image and identity to challenge the status quo – socially, culturally and politically. Singer, songwriter and dancer P!nk began performing aged 14 in 1995, adopting her stage-name with ambition and flair. The artist continues to push boundaries on and off stage, stretching the limits through acrobatic stage performances and shattering expectations with her bold style and rebellious spirit (p. 57).

By the new millennium the term diva has become widely used to describe all-encompassing powerful singers 'with attitude' from a variety of genres. The media often choose to dwell on the diva's behaviour and to portray their careers and creativity in a negative light, thus reinforcing diva clichés. Journalists describe global megastars such as Whitney Houston, Mariah Carey and Madonna as 'out of control', 'scary' or 'outrageous' rather

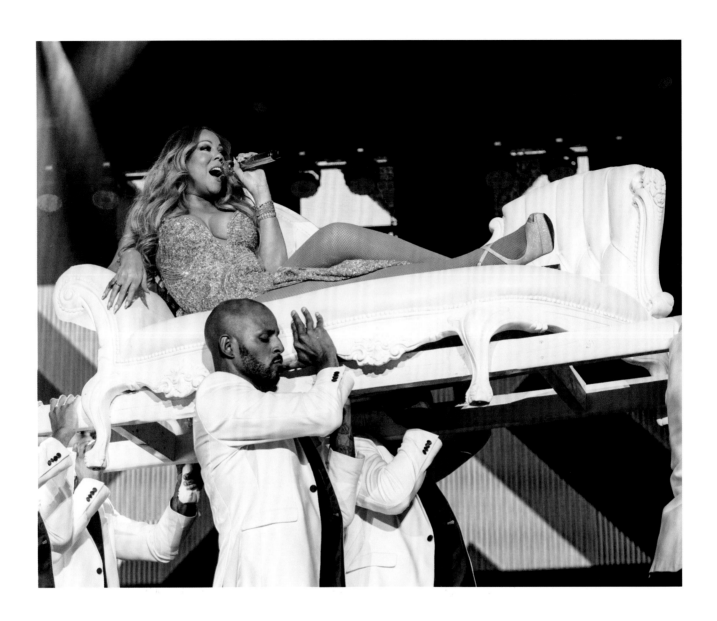

Mariah Carey performing at the Essence
Festival, New Orleans, 2016

than focusing on their artistry and exceptional talent. As a result, the modern diva must constantly challenge public perceptions and find new ways to own the term.

Mariah Carey has developed an empowered response to counter the media representation of her diva persona. In 2021 the *Daily Mail* declared that 'Mariah Carey adds fuel to diva rumours after revealing she required SIX men to carry her 70lb gown's train' and shared stories of 'rumours of diva-like behaviour throughout her career, which sees her bathe in milk, reportedly turn up to events up to four hours late and demand that her trailer is filled with stuffed lambs'.[51] Accomplished artist, songwriter, vocal arranger and music producer, Carey confidently took the diva concept back into her own hands: 'You think in the grand scheme of things in my life that really matters to me, being called a diva?'[52] With her exceptional five-octave vocal range and multifaceted career, Carey stated that 'I come from a true diva: My mother is an opera singer. And that's a real diva, you know…'.[53]

Tragically some divas have not been able to withstand the public scrutiny of their lives. In his recent biography of Whitney Houston, Gerrick Kennedy reflected on the impact of the intrusive media obsession with Houston's personal life, from her addiction to her sexuality: 'It's a reminder that if we'd treated her differently, we could have had a different Whitney… Maybe if she hadn't experienced the judgment and the shame, other choices would have been made.'[54]

As well as re-imagining traditional media like film, video and stage, liberated divas of the twenty-first century also draw on new technologies and media, from Instagram and TikTok to immersive audio and mixed reality, bringing them closer to their fans. After Priyanka Chopra was crowned Miss World in the 2000s her career has seen a meteoric rise across disciplines. Since then she become a leading lady in Bollywood and in Hollywood, a style icon, singer, tech entrepreneur, producer and philanthropist, reflecting how the diva on the global stage has power and agency to occupy both traditional and new spaces.

The ultimate multifaceted artist, Lady Gaga thrives in a constantly evolving creative universe, channelling her vision into scenography in both the virtual and the physical realms. Gaga seamlessly shifts between different worlds, from award-winning Hollywood blockbusters to metamorphic stage productions. In her words:

*I am an artist and I have the ability and the free will to choose the way the world will envision me. Don't ever let a soul in the world tell you that you can't be exactly who you are.*[55]

Staying true to yourself is the mantra of multitalented diva Lizzo, who champions body positivity and is a vocal proponent of self-love, encouraging fans to celebrate themselves as they are. This spirit is also exmplified by global phenomenon Rihanna (pp. 115–21). Today's divas are reclaiming their inner goddesses, engaging audiences across many arenas, from the Super Bowl to the catwalk, from politics to the boardroom, from motherhood to the high street.

Whether contesting sexual, social, political or economic norms, divas are a force for change in society. Black women performers have the additional challenge of fighting for women's empowerment and independence while also fighting against racism. In the 2019 documentary film *Homecoming*, Beyoncé draws inspiration from a range of Black intellectuals and leaders, including Audre Lorde, continuing to use her global platform as an artist to elevate the female voice and champion Black empowerment. From her 2013 song 'Flawless', which samples Chimamanda Ngozi Adichie's *We Should All be Feminists*[56] to 'Formation', an anthem for Black power and resilience, Beyoncé shows the world how a diva is a leader and a game-changer – assertive and courageous.

Divas throughout history are a creation and a fantasy, by turns intriguing, complex, exuberant, delicate and political, but always individual, self-made, enduring and creative. As we redefine the diva today and reassess the performer's legacy, we must shift the negative to the positive: the unpredictable becomes creative, the aggressive becomes powerful, the self-obsessed is worshipped, the materialist is an entrepreneur, the narcissist is self-aware, the control-freak is a perfectionist, the rebel is a game-changer and the exhibitionist is an artist.

Today the diva continues to be seen from myriad perspectives. The term is constantly being redefined and reclaimed by the performers themselves, their fans and wider society. Female stars in our own time engage overtly with the idea of the diva in songs, concept albums and creative style. Annie Lennox owned the term in her debut

Priyanka Chopra performs at a show after
the Twenty20 cricket match between India
and South Africa, Durban, 2011

Album cover for Annie Lennox's *Diva*,
photographed by Satoshi Saikusa, designed
by Laurence Stevens. Sony Records, 1992

Album cover for *Fairuz*. Voix de l'Orient,
1988

studio album, *Diva*, in 1992; in 2009 Beyoncé declared in an eponymous R&B song that the diva is a female version of a hustler; and in 2018 contenders in the reality show *RuPaul's Drag Race* competed to impersonate divas from Diana Ross to Cher. The diva concept can be playful and entertaining as well as a symbol of empowerment and strength for women and for a variety of marginalized and disenfranchised groups: the duality of many divas – their struggles and expressive femininity alongside their powerful sense of self – is often admired by LGBTQ+ communities.

At the heart of the concept of diva in this book, and the exhibition it accompanies, is an artist with voice, vision and attitude who creates a deep connection with their followers. Several key characteristics reappear again and again over time, and the ways in which these traits have flourished in the past seventy years is explored in the chapters that follow. Sarah Bernhardt's inventive, radical and canny use of her image is echoed in the more recent rebel divas surveyed here by Lucy O'Brien and Sasha Geffen. Marie Lloyd's fight for workers' rights sees a counterpoint in the voices against racial injustice in Jaqueline Springer's chapter. Veronica Castro explores the contemporary equivalents of the magnificently successful Adelina Patti. Keith Lodwick reveals how costume and style were as important to the diva in twentieth-century Hollywood and the contemporary drag queen as they were to the nineteenth-century Italian opera star. And Miranda Sawyer reveals that to be truly ubiquitous, as the diva is, requires negotiating a tightrope between the public and the private in ways that can be fruitful or destructive.

Powerful aspects of the diva that continue to shape our conceptions today have evolved from the challenges and triumphs of their predecessors. Together they create a constellation of idols and worshippers in this majestic and powerful Divadom.

**I will always be as difficult as necessary to achieve the best.**

Maria Callas

**I am my own experiment, I am my own work of art.**

Madonna

**When I decided to be a singer, my mother warned me I'd be alone a lot. Basically we all are. Loneliness comes with life.**

Whitney Houston

**Hollywood is a place where they'll pay you a thousand dollars for a kiss and fifty cents for your soul.**

Marilyn Monroe

**A true diva is graceful and talented, and strong and fearless and brave, and someone with humility.**

Beyoncé

I walk fast. Keep moving. Always be a moving target. Marilyn Monroe taught me that.

Liza Minnelli

Listen, baby, I sing for my supper. I don't have to cook it as well.

Shirley Bassey

I think women want freedom. They want to be empowered. They want hope. They want all the things I want. That's why they identify with me.

Rihanna

I have learned how to fight. I have never been scared of anyone. I am quite fearless.

Lata Mangeshkar

I've been pronounced dead and I've read my own obituaries. And they were the best reviews I ever read.

Elizabeth Taylor

Beyoncé performing at Glastonbury Festival,
2011. Photograph by Denis O'Regan

Prince performing at Wembley Arena,
London, 1986. Photograph by David Corio

Lizzo out in New York City wearing Viktor & Rolf, 2021

P!nk performs at Madison Square Garden during her 'Funhouse' tour, New York City, 2009

Costume designed by Sandy Powell for
Elton John on the occasion of his 50th
birthday party, 1997

# A Star is Born:
# Creating the Diva

Keith Lodwick

# 'I am big, it's the picture that got small.'[1]

Creating and performing the diva requires talent, dedication, endurance and the pursuit of perfection. Whether we gaze up at a huge projected cinematic image, experience a performance at Caesars Palace in Las Vegas or are in the audience at Glastonbury, our diva goddesses require elevation and worship from afar. We are, as Norma Desmond in *Sunset Boulevard* (1950) reminds us, 'those wonderful people out there in the dark'.

Desmond's final moments in *Sunset Boulevard* have entered the annals of cinema history and secured the immortality of one of the greatest characters of the silver screen. The film was set in Hollywood; its theatrical equivalent, New York's Broadway, was the backdrop for *All About Eve* released the same year. Starring Gloria Swanson (1899–1983) and Bette Davis respectively, the films created two larger-than-life characters in Norma Desmond and Margo Channing. They later reached new audiences on stage and endured in popular culture as both were later made into musicals: *All About Eve* became *Applause* (1970) and Sunset Boulevard opened under its original title in London in 1993. Glenn Close, who won a Tony Award for the Broadway transfer of the latter in 1994, called Norma Desmond 'one of the great cinematic characters'.[2]

Desmond's visual appearance was created by Swanson and Edith Head, whose career was in the ascendency in the late 1940s, having just won the Best Costume Design Oscar for *Samson and Delilah* (1949). Swanson (who had created her own clothing label) had learned the visual tricks of the trade to make herself appear taller on screen (she was just 4 ft 11 in/1.5 m tall), giving the illusion of height by lengthening her skirts and dropping the waistline. She had been part of the creation of Hollywood's Golden Age, yet was now appearing in one of the most subversive anti-Hollywood films of the era. She had witnessed the global popularity and growth of cinema as a visual medium, changing the nature of fame and public recognition forever. By 1950 the Hollywood studio system was beginning to unravel.

While film historians may have viewed Swanson as the epitome of the fading silent film star, at the same time as she was making *Sunset Boulevard* she had her own television series, was managing her own fashion brand and was also publicly advocating healthy eating. After her film career was largely over, Swanson had diversified and was an early influencer, successfully multitasking in various creative and business arenas. Unlike her most famous character, she was not nostalgic: her granddaughter recalls that 'she never looked to the past, she only looked forward. She was completely different to the character she played in *Sunset*'.[3]

Bette Davis's career was also in transition in 1950. The previous year, after 18 years at Warner Bros., where she had been dubbed 'the fifth Warner Brother',[4] Davis committed the film industry's ultimate crime: she had had 'three flops in a row'.[5] As she drove out of the Warner Bros. lot on her final day, the actor recalled, 'no one said goodbye, and no one sent a leaving card, I drove past all those sound stages that were built from money earned from my films'.[6] With echoes of the narrative of *Sunset Boulevard*, Davis was already being described as 'washed up'.[7] But she was about to embark on an extraordinary project and, like Swanson, play a role that would cement her image forever.

Gloria Swanson in *Sunset Boulevard*, poster, 1950

# 'Fasten your seat belts, it's going to be a bumpy night' [8]

Elevated on a staircase, Margo Channing delivers this oft-quoted line. Davis credited director and writer Joseph L. Mankiewicz for 'resurrecting me from the dead',[9] yet her performance as Channing was built on a career playing disruptive, provocative and compelling characters. She strove for realism on the screen and changed the way that women were presented in film. Off screen, she challenged the male-constructed studio system and began the fight to end the 'tyranny of the seven-year contract'.[10]

After she won an Oscar for Best Actress in *Dangerous* (1935), Warner Bros. forced Davis into mediocre films; she went on strike and was duly suspended (a common practice during this era). In retaliation, she sued Warner Bros. Although the studio won and she was forced to return to work, she later remarked: 'I lost the battle but won the war'.[11] But she had put the wheels in motion. In 1944 her friend and contemporary at Warner Bros. Olivia de Havilland (1916–2020) also took the studio to court over her contract – and won. In revenge, Jack Warner tried to have De Havilland blacklisted but the actor prevailed and went on to win two Oscars for Best Actress while freelancing between studios. Thus Davis and De Havilland had paved the way for the modern freedom of movement for actors.

As with *Sunset Boulevard*, Edith Head had a role to play in the creation of Margo Channing, Davis's most famous character. When Davis discussed the role with Mankiewicz, he told her that 'Margo Channing is a woman who treats a mink coat like a poncho'.[12] Head later recalled meeting Davis for the fitting:

*Bette walks in like a small, disciplined cyclone. She shows you how she is going to do the part, how she is throwing herself on a bed, sits on a desk or whirls around and Bette tells me that is the way I want the clothes to act.*[13]

Due to hurried pre-production work, when Davis tried on her signature costume it slipped down off her shoulders. Head realized that the measurements had been done incorrectly, however Davis suggested that it would look better if her shoulders were exposed. Head's happy accident became one of her most famous designs.

Behind the scenes of Hollywood's all-male coterie of directors, Mankiewicz was warned that Bette Davis 'will destroy you, then she, and not you, will direct'.[14] But Mankiewicz ignored the advice and found the opposite: the professionally prepared actor, Davis was 'always ready on set, she knew not only her lines, but everyone else's'.[15] When *All About Eve* was released it was a major critical and commercial success, garnering a record 14 Oscar nominations and winning six, including Best Film.

Bette Davis continued to work on high-profile films until her death, giving a daring and provocative performance in *Whatever Happened to Baby Jane?* (1962) and appearing in the all-star *Death on the Nile* (1978). However, her creative influence and imprint on popular culture extended beyond Hollywood. In 1974 Donna Weiss and Jackie DeShannon wrote 'Bette Davis Eyes'. Recorded by Kim Carnes in 1981, it was on the US Billboard Hot 100 for

Bette Davis as Margo Channing in *All About Eve*, 1950

nine weeks and became a number one hit worldwide. The official video featured Carnes singing in the foreground in front of a silhouette of Bette Davis as Margo Channing. Madonna, inspired by the women who had shaped Hollywood and American culture, name-checked Davis in her 1990 hit song 'Vogue'.

Davis's appeal to her audiences was diverse and the growing visibility of her loyal gay following began to make itself known in the late 1950s and '60s. When she appeared on Broadway in *Night of the Iguana*, the predominately gay audience 'went wild in appreciation' when she came on stage.[16] Davis told LGBT magazine *The Advocate* in 1977, 'as conceited as it may sound, I think a great deal of it has to do with their approval of my work'.[17] Her close friend the writer Dotson Rader reflected that 'she realized that one of the reasons for the longevity of her career, was her gay

audience'.[18] Female impersonator Charles Busch, who took inspiration from Davis, reflected on her ultimate appeal to gay audiences:

> All About Eve *is one of those handful of movies you have to see to get your gay card, with Sunset Boulevard ... These are powerful women, fighting for their rights in a straight man's world, gay men can identify with this.*[19]

Best remembered for their career-defining roles, Gloria Swanson and Bette Davis belong to a group of women whose careers, personalities and screen characters have endured and shaped modern popular culture. Yet at some point in their careers both were labelled 'divas', a derogatory term when used by male studio heads, producers and directors. Both actors were aware of the connotation of being 'difficult and demanding' as they strove for perfection, but they both fought to raise the bar for themselves and those who followed. Their influence has produced ripples across every aspect of culture – film and television, musicals, academic research, impersonation and homage.

Irene Sharaff dressing Elizabeth Taylor in 1961–2 for the film *Cleopatra* (directed by Joseph L. Mankiewicz), 1963

# A star is reborn

While Swanson and Davis were creating their most enduring performances, two other actors were also at a crossroads in 1950: Judy Garland (1922–1969) and Elizabeth Taylor (1932–2011). In the late 1930s and '40s, Garland was MGM's biggest film star: the studio built musicals around her and for her. It also controlled all aspects of her public and private life, as she recalled:

*After filming was finished, they would take us to the studio hospital and knock us cold with sleeping pills. Then after four hours, they'd wake us up with pep-pills so we could work another 72 hours in a row.*[20]

Having worked Garland into the ground, in 1950 MGM terminated her contract. But her talent, charisma and drive enabled her to continue: abandoning Hollywood, and the studio that had 'robbed her of her childhood',[21] Garland returned to her stage roots as a singer and vaudeville performer. Re-energized, she spent the early 1950s performing and reconnecting with her audience, 'then came the wonderful opportunity to appear at the London Palladium [in 1951], where I can truthfully say Judy Garland was reborn'.[22]

Hollywood wooed her back in 1954 to star in the musical remake of *A Star is Born* (the second of four versions). The film was a critical and commercial success and brought her first Oscar nomination for Best Actress. Garland's subsequent return to live performance at New York's Carnegie Hall in 1961 (overleaf) was described as 'the greatest night in show business history'.[23] Her magnetism allowed her to connect with individuals through live performance, and the reach of film was global.

Like Bette Davis, Judy Garland became aware of her audience demographic. In 1967 *Time* magazine dubbed her 'the Elvis for homosexuals ... The boys in the tight trousers roll their eyes, tear at their hair and practically levitate from their seats during Garland's performance'.[24]

The adoption of the diva by the LGBTQ+ community is partly the legacy of Garland's performances in *The Wizard of Oz* (1939), *A Star is Born* and her live appearances. But in time her well-documented turbulent private life also made her a gay idol: Garland's appeal is also about survival. In an era of gay oppression, it wasn't enough to be talented and famous; gay people idolized those they saw as fellow survivors. Garland's well-documented problems with drink, drugs and men (she was married five times) have made her an icon to the gay community to this day. The roots of this connection go back much further and are embedded in gay history itself. The term 'a friend of Dorothy' to mean a (male) homosexual has an unknown origin but may be derived from *The Road to Oz* (1909) by L. Frank Baum, sequel to his first novel, *The Wonderful Wizard of Oz* (1900). The book introduces readers to Polychrome (daughter of the rainbow), who, upon meeting Dorothy's travelling companions, exclaims, 'you have some queer friends, Dorothy'.[25]

Garland died in London on 22 June 1969, aged just 47. On the eve of her funeral service in New York the Stonewall riots took place in Greenwich Village, sparking the beginning of the modern gay liberation movement. Activist Sylvia Rivera (1951–2002), who was present at Stonewall on the day of the riots, recalled people being disturbed at Garland's death at such a young age; when the inevitable police raid occurred, she said, 'we were not going to take any more shit from the police'.[26]

Whether Garland's early death ignited a gay uprising from oppression is debatable, but the two events have become entwined in LGBTQ+ history. She left a lasting imprint on popular culture and she continues to feature in books, plays and films. In 2019 Renée Zellweger won an Oscar for Best Actress portraying her in the film *Judy*.

Garland's daughter, Liza Minnelli, carved out her own career between film, television and live performance (overleaf). The desire to entertain, for audience adoration and approval, was in the family's DNA, as Minnelli recalled:

*I had researched the family tree, noting her own destiny in the process, my family's been in show business since the 1700s, I traced them. I'm bred to this, like a racehorse.*[27]

For Minnelli, it required grit and determination to emerge from the long shadow of her world-famous mother, as she discovered when they appeared together on Garland's TV show:

*One minute I was on stage with my mother, the next moment it was Judy Garland. One minute she smiled at*

Judy Garland reaching out to her adoring
audience, Carnegie Hall, New York, 1961

Liza Minnelli performing at the Tony Awards,
New York, 1984

*me, the next she was the lioness that owned the stage and found someone invading her territory, the killer instinct of a performer had come out in her.*[28]

During the 1940s Garland's contemporary at MGM was Elizabeth Taylor, whose career was also controlled by the studio. In the 1950s Taylor began to make the transition from juvenile leads to major roles in a series of dramas, including *Giant* (1956) and *Cat on a Hot Tin Roof* (1958), yet she was frustrated by the studio control of her career. When she was finally released from MGM in 1960, Taylor began to build independently on her reputation and brand; in that process, 'all roads led to Rome'.[29]

When Taylor was telephoned by the producer of *Cleopatra* to ask if she would consider playing the title role, she jokingly remarked 'I'll do it for a million dollars'.[30] Her statement would create the modern film star phenomenon: she was the first actor – male or female – to be paid a million dollars for a single role. Like Bette Davis, Taylor championed independence and negotiated contracts that were tailored to her, with the approval of director, costume designer and cinematographer – and paved the way for other actors to do the same. Her business acumen also ensured Taylor's ownership of the creative visualization of *Cleopatra*. She had written in to her contract that the film must be shot in the 70mm film format 'Todd AO', a system that she owned, having inherited it from her husband, Mike Todd, after he died in a plane crash in 1958. She also negotiated 10 per cent of the *Cleopatra* profits.

In spring 1962 the filming of Cleopatra's triumphal entry into Rome took place, introduced by troupes of dancing girls, elephants, archers, chariots and trumpet players. Elizabeth Taylor was figuratively and literally on top of the world, seated on a black marble sphinx pulled by over three hundred extras. Her costume, designed by Irene Sharaff (p. 68), incorporated a cape adorned with 24-carat gold, patterned with the wings of a phoenix; her headdress was equally resplendent. The cultural impact of *Cleopatra* was immense: it was the highest grossing film of 1963 and one of the most successful films of the 1960s, and Taylor's 10 per cent share of the profits enabled her to choose her subsequent roles and have total control over her career.

Alongside her creative work, Taylor used her fame as a platform for humanitarian causes more than any other twentieth-century film star. She emerged as a powerful force for compassion at a time when industry colleagues refused to risk their fame on a cause shrouded with stigma. In the early 1980s the AIDS health crisis became a deadly global pandemic and the backlash against the gay community was widespread. The right-wing media depicted the disease as a 'gay plague', AIDS decimated gay communities and in 1985 the world was shocked when Taylor's *Giant* co-star and friend, Rock Hudson, died of the disease. Taylor visited AIDS hospices, held gala fund-raising events and appealed to US Congress for funding. In recognition of her work, in 1993 she was awarded the Academy's Jean Hersholt Humanitarian Award.

# Costuming the modern diva

Costume has enabled the diva to embrace her independence and reinvention. It was seeing the work of Edith Head, who had worked with Bette Davis for *Sunset Boulevard* and *All About Eve*, and Irene Sharaff, who had designed for Judy Garland in *Meet Me in St Louis* and *A Star is Born* and won an Oscar for *Cleopatra*, that inspired Bob Mackie to become a costume designer. Mackie had always sketched and designed clothes and had grown up watching the films of the Golden Age of Hollywood. When he arrived at Paramount Pictures as a sketch artist, Edith Head took an interest in his work and eventually hired him. This led to his first professional television job, assisting Ray Aghayan designing *The Judy Garland Show* (1963–4); Aghayan would become his long-term partner. For one of the shows Aghayan designed the 'poppy dress' for Garland, referencing *The Wizard of Oz*.

As Hollywood films in the early 1970s reflected national economic decline and political upheaval, television offered escapist and highly popular variety shows. It was women who dominated this arena, with Carol Burnett and Mary Tyler Moore (1936–2017) becoming pioneers in their field, producing, starring and writing their own shows. With Burnett, Mackie formed one of his most successful partnerships. He designed all 11 seasons of her hugely popular variety show, which included sketches that parodied Hollywood films.

It was in the medium of TV that singer, actor, philanthropist and global icon Cher was able to take control of her career. Long before the trend of monosyllabic names for pop stars came into vogue, Cher was challenging stereotypes of race, age and beauty. Over the course of her career she has reinvited herself in every decade: hippie in the 1960s, queen of the TV variety show in the 1970s and rock diva in the 1980s. In the late 1960s, as one half of the pop music duo Sonny and Cher, she was in the shadow of her husband Sonny Bono, who controlled her career

> ... for five years before I left him, and I wanted to leave, but the [TV] show was so popular that I was afraid and when I did leave, he told me, 'America will hate you, you'll never work again'.[31]

Inspired by the golden age stars Bette Davis, Judy Garland and Katharine Hepburn, Cher found independent fame and empowerment on television, while revolutionizing the variety show format. Her transformation was aided by Mackie's costume creations. When she played Cleopatra in a TV special on the history of women's clothes in 1975, she and Mackie had the opportunity to costume a character immortalized on film over decades by Theda Bara (1917), Claudette Colbert (1934), Vivien Leigh (1945) and Elizabeth Taylor (1963).

Cher made the transition from television into film in the early 1980s in a series of unglamorous and challenging roles. In *Silkwood* (1983) she played a factory worker in a nuclear production facility. For *Mask* (1985) Cher received the Cannes Film Festival Award for Best Actress for her portrayal of real-life Rusty Dennis, mother of Rocky Dennis, who had the disfiguring disease lionitis.

When the Academy of Motion Picture Arts and Sciences failed to recognize this performance in the Best Actress category, Cher rebelled against the system. When presenting the Oscar for Best Supporting Actor, she wore a stunning black costume with feathered headdress, designed by Mackie, which she nicknamed her 'revenge dress',[32] and remarked to the audience: 'as you can see, I did receive my Academy booklet on how to dress like a serious actress'.[33] She was disrupting the dress code and the moment became one of the highlights of the 1986 Oscar ceremony. But Cher soon cemented her acting credentials, winning an Oscar for *Moonstruck* (1987). Like Taylor, Cher lent her voice to a range of humanitarian projects, including PFLAG (Parents, Families and Friends of Lesbians and Gays). Her liberation from male control of her career in the 1970s helped her carve out a model of third-wave feminism with an emphasis on individual empowerment and diversity.

Shirley Bassey made her US debut in Las Vegas in 1957 and performed at the Carnegie Hall in 1965, following in the footsteps of Judy Garland. She was already established as a major singing and recording performer in the UK by the late 1950s, but global success came through her association with the James Bond film franchise. 'Goldfinger' (1964), the first of three Bond themes that Bassey recorded, set a high bar in terms of production, recording and performance. Subsequent Bond theme songs are referenced against this towering fusion of performer and music.

In the 1970s Bassey expanded her audience with her own television series for the BBC, occupying the coveted

Shirley Bassey at Glastonbury Festival,
costume by Julien MacDonald, 2007

Left:
Sketch by Bob Mackie of Egyptian ensemble
for Cher for the launch of her perfume,
Uninhibited, 1988

Saturday evening slot as she continued to adapt and explore new possibilities in music and performance. In 2007 she engaged with a younger demographic at the Glastonbury Festival, the pre-eminent music festival in Europe. Dressed in a Julien MacDonald pink gown with diamanté-studded wellington boots, Bassey arrived at the event in a helicopter and performed her most enduring hits. In the audience was Guardian music journalist Alex Needham, who declared that 'this Glastonbury will forever be known as the one that Shirley did'.[34]

In 1998 an annual series of concerts, 'VH1 Divas', was created to support the Save The Music Foundation.[35] Aretha Franklin, Mariah Carey, Shania Twain, Gloria Estefan and Celine Dion inaugurated the first concert. The following year Cher, Tina Turner and special guest 'divo' – or male diva – Elton John performed. Over the course of the next ten years, Donna Summer, Miley Cyrus, Shakira, Debbie Harry, Whitney Houston, Beyoncé, and Adele have also taken part. The 2000 show was dedicated to one performer, Diana Ross, who requested that the concert be recorded rather than performed live to ensure that she had time for her costume changes. During her tribute show Ross frequently abandoned the stage to wander among the audience at Madison Square Garden. In their tribute renditions, Mariah Carey, Donna Summer, Destiny's Child, Faith Hill and RuPaul all hailed Ross as the 'Supremist Supreme'. Ross wore a spangled outfit that matched Mariah Carey's own during their performance of 'Baby Love'. But Ross provided the biggest moment during the event – a reunion with former Supremes Lynda Laurence and Scherrie Payne to perform 'You Keep Me Hanging On'.

Ross and Mackie have had a long collaboration. The TV special *G.I.T. (Gettin' It Together) on Broadway*, starring Diana Ross and The Supremes and The Temptations, was broadcast in 1969 (overleaf). Ross's homage channelled Garland's 'Born in a Trunk' sequence from *A Star is Born*; scenes from *My Fair Lady*, *Mame* and *South Pacific*; Barbra Streisand's 'People' from *Funny Girl*; and finished with 'Everything's Coming Up Roses' from *Gypsy*. Mackie was instructed to create every costume as if Ross 'had created the role originally on Broadway'.[36] Two months after the broadcast Ross left The Supremes to forge her own career. In 1972 she requested that Mackie re-design her costumes when she was portraying Billie Holiday in *Lady Sings the*

Sketch by Bob Mackie for the iconic 'Flame
Dress' for Tina Turner, 1977

Left:
Diana Ross dressed for a television special
*G.I.T. On Broadway*, wearing a voluminous
wig and minidress designed by Bob Mackie,
1969

*Blues,* for which she received an Oscar nomination for
Best Actress.

One of Mackie's most iconic designs is the 'flame dress',
worn by performers including Cher, Diana Ross, Tina Turner
and RuPaul; Beyoncé wore a version for her tribute to Tina
Turner at the 2005 Kennedy Centre Honors. The costume
has come to symbolize the diva emerging from a blazing
sun, like a goddess, with the flames creating new life. For
Turner, Cher and Ross, reinvention has become part of their
longevity and costume is central to that reinvigoration.

# Empowering your inner diva

Participant at the Diana Ross tribute, RuPaul has spent his career performing, re-creating and paying homage to the diva. He became widely known with the single 'Supermodel (You Better Work)' in 1993. Through his multi-award-winning reality show *RuPaul's Drag Race* (2009 onwards) both he and the contestants have kept the tradition of the diva alive through costume, attitude and performance. Bob Mackie was a guest judge for the first episode and has appeared several times.

Contestants in the show have performed biopic musical tributes ('Rusicals') to Cher and Madonna and have had fashion challenges to dress like their icons. Lady Gaga herself appeared as a judge for 'The Night of 1000 Gagas' in 2022. The contestants are also encouraged to capture the essence of the divas, with personality and mannerisms being as important as humour. RuPaul is careful to distinguish between his gender and his performance identity – he appears both in and out of drag in each episode – and believes that we all have an 'inner diva' that can be brought out through drag.

RuPaul has shifted drag from an underground sub-culture into the mainstream. LGBTQ+ history is referenced throughout his show to emphasize its importance, particularly to younger contestants. He refers to his female best friends as his 'Judys' (after Garland) and his admiration of powerful women and pop culture references has educated a new generation of performers on the shoulders of the divas who came before them. Whether it be Norma Desmond or Margo Channing on a staircase, or Shirley Bassey or Cher (in *Mamma Mia! Here We Go Again*) arriving in a helicopter, these women are fully in charge of their impact on audiences. We gaze up at them, figures elevated to a higher plane, enthralled by their majesty, glamour and domination. We may just be 'the people out there in the dark', in the words of Norma Desmond, but performing the diva not only empowers them: it also empowers us.

RuPaul wearing a Bob Mackie flame dress at the APLA Commitment to Life VIII AIDS benefit, Los Angles, 1995

Still from *RuPaul's Drag Race All Stars*, season 3, episode 2: *Divas Live!*, February 2018

Cher, Elton John and Diana Ross at the
Rock Music Awards, Santa Monica Civic
Auditorium, 1975

Sketch by Bob Mackie for an ensemble worn
by Cher to the Rock Music Awards, 1975

Cher

# Backlash Blues: Voices for Change

Jacqueline Springer

Denied the opportunity to sing in
Washington's Constitution Hall on the
grounds of her race, Marian Anderson instead
performed to approximately 75,000 people
at the Lincoln Memorial, 1939.
Photograph by Tom McAvoy

In 1958 police raided Tennessee's Highlander Folk School, a noted institution that served as both an educational facility and a civil rights hub.[1] Jamila Jones was among those subjected to the raid. Jamila, a 'veteran' of the Montgomery bus boycott two years prior, had been at Highlander for 'activist training': learning how to endure and minimize impacts of the intimidation, verbal taunts and physical violence attracted by advocating for racial equality. Jamila Jones was just 14 years old. Years later she recalled the experience:

Policemen from the city came in ... they came in and turned out all the lights. So we were in complete darkness that night. We were just there, wherever we were at the time when the lights went out, that's where we sat. So all these policemen came in. All we could see basically is the billy club waving and the butts of their guns – you could see it shining in their holster. They told us to sit – told us to stay seated – to be quiet or whatever.

And something [within] said ... 'We are not afraid.' Everybody started singing: 'We are not...' and you could hear people come in [singing] and we got louder and louder with singing that verse until one of the policemen came and he said to me, 'If you have to sing,' – and he was actually shaking – 'do you have to sing so loud?' I could not believe it. Here these people had all the guns. The billy clubs. The power, we thought. And he was asking me, with a shake, if I would not sing so loud.

It was that time that I really understood the power of our music. How powerful it was that it unnerved him so much that that he had to come and ask that I not sing so loud. And I can just tell you that I got louder and louder.

---

Ella Fitzgerald in the UK with promotional photographs, 1958. Photograph by Harry Hammond
V&A: S.11161-2009

Our voices blended that night to the point of complete harmony and beauty and from then on, I knew exactly how powerful our songs were.[2]

The verse Jamila led others through was from the well-known folk/worker song turned gospel hymn 'We Shall Overcome', which began its expressed life in the first-person singular: 'I Shall Overcome'. Folk songs, worker songs, Negro spirituals, gospel, freedom songs, all, irrespective of formal classification, are odes, appeals, triumphant I-told-you-so unifiers of the enslaved, the labourer, the beleaguered, the oppressed, the believer, the faithful, the redeemed, the inspired.

Within their stanzas and choruses these songs relay a pressing need to be heard, and for what is heard be addressed. Hope is relayed in personal and social change coming to bear as a result of being listened to; by listeners being moved to change personal or collective circumstance. Hope resides in the hearts and on the tongues of those who sing.

These songs, hymns and abridged choruses possess tenuously balanced dual narratives: the subject of woe (or the people responsible for it) is outlined; the retelling of woe (often cushioned by biblical references and parallels) relays its impact. Performed contemporaneously, these known songs, hymns and abridged choruses reflect modern lived truths. They substantiate horrors, unhappiness and frustrations. They seek that the weight of the relayed experiences be lifted from the shoulders of those who know that the weight need not be borne at all.

Children (like Jamila), growing up confined by social, racial and gendered inequalities, recognize the narrative balance held within such musical genres to the degree that they can instinctively edit material at will. This allows them to musically speak to and within situations that they should never witness or endure. These skills are acquired and implemented because racism and intersecting social inequalities have pervaded long enough for musical canons to emerge in response to them.

In his landmark publication The Souls of Black Folk, W.E.B. Du Bois, influential historian, sociologist, equal rights campaigner and founding member of the National Association of the Advancement of Coloured People (NAACP), grouped such types of music under the collective

Billie Holiday with Frank Newton and his
Café Society Orchestra, recording *Strange
Fruit* for Commodore Records at New York's
World Broadcasting Studio, 1939

Following pages:
Billie Holiday at her only ever London
appearance at the Albert Hall, with Jack
Parnell band backing, 1954. Photograph by
Harry Hammond.
V&A: S.7617-2009

moniker 'sorrow songs', given that their expression and dissemination on American soil owed their descendancy to African antecedents – a lineage violently interrupted by the transatlantic slave trade:

> I know that these songs are the articulate message of the Slave to the world. They are the music of an unhappy people, of the children of disappointment; they tell of death and suffering and unvoiced longing toward a truer world, of misty wanderings and hidden ways.

> The songs are indeed the siftings of the centuries; the music is far more ancient than the words, and in it we can trace here and there signs of development.[3]

At 14 when she realized the power of music, Jamila Jones was younger than Ella Fitzgerald and Miriam Makeba (1932–2008), the same age as Elenore Harris (1915–1959, later Billie Holiday) but older than Eunice Kathleen Waymon (1933–2003, later Nina Simone) and Aretha Franklin (1942–2018) when they in turn realized that the music they expressed held power. Like Jamila, this changed their world-view. But unlike Jamila, through their expression of music, the direction of their lives and perceptions of popular music in North America, South Africa and Western Europe would be forever altered.

Nina Simone was just three and a half years old when she accompanied her mother, a Methodist minister, to churches to provide musical accompaniment for her revival services. Aretha was aged ten when she settled into the travelling ministry schedule of her father, Reverend C.L. Franklin, singing with a depth of feeling beyond her years during church services dominated by his sermons. The late Revd Franklin remains one of the most revered (and controversial) Black ministers in America. His oratory skills and theological knowledge were so vaunted that he was not only a peer and friend of Dr Martin Luther King Jr, he also organized the 1963 Detroit Freedom March for him – the protest that preceded the March on Washington by two months. The Reverend and his daughter had, of course, no way of knowing that her musical accompaniment was the vocal training for her eventual rule – as 'the Queen of Soul'– over a global musical kingdom.

Much has been made of the textures of Billie Holiday

and Ella Fitzgerald's voices. Billie Holiday's is a scorched ember that radiates within the ears and possesses a knowing, gurgling warmth and lustre. Primal descriptions have determined to sexualize it, rendering its depth and ruggedness sensual. But Holiday's vocal richness also harboured a fractured heaviness; a pathos. When employed to perform songs in protest against domestic terrorism – as she did in the song 'Strange Fruit' – her dark, off-kilter pacing provided a vivid picture of the horror of hatred and the deaths it pursued. The memorable starkness of 'Strange Fruit' lies in its ability to both compare and distinguish what it presents: how the public execution of Black men, boys, women and girls, their hanging from trees, was accomplished in opposition to that which naturally occurs in nature: the perennial rebirth of life *from* trees. The evocative depiction of this abuse of human nature and the natural world by the interjection of vicious, violent racist injustice further revealed that in the 86 years between 1882 and 1968, 3,346 African Americans were killed by this method of supremacist vigilantism.[4] The NAACP flew a flag outside its New York headquarters bearing the statement 'A Black Man was Lynched Yesterday' as daily reminder of the nationwide murders. The flag flew for 18 years.[5]

Holiday unveiled 'Strange Fruit' at New York's Café Society nightclub – apt, given its integrationist intent and that its owner, Barney Josephson, had brought the song to Holiday's attention. It was originally a poem entitled 'Bitter Fruit', written by communist and activist Abel Meeropol, who also worked under the pseudonym Lewis Allan. Holiday was initially reluctant to sing or record it. By the time she did, its title had altered and its staging settled upon: Holiday would close her set with it and no distractions – no serving of drinks or food – would take place during her performance. The imposed immutability of the audience would honour the subject (and by extension, the victims). The audience would see the 'blood on the leaves', the torsos 'swinging in the Southern breeze', because her delivery would be so pointed that it was all but sermonized.

'Strange Fruit' attracted far-reaching acclaim as well as defensive, censorious opposition. Holiday's record label refused to record and release the song but granted her permission to do so independently. Holiday and her

band received threats against performing it. Many radio stations across America had exclusionary racial and stylistic playlist policies which severely limited its playtime, and it was banned from BBC radio broadcasts in the UK.[6] Despite this, the song became a commercial success, eventually selling a million copies. For some, Holiday had become, performatively, 'political': a singer who not only had the 'audacity' to exercise her talent by beautifully highlighting heinous acts of political and social concern, but a Black woman who had roused national interest in the continued existence of these racist acts and the top-down political inaction in preventing or adequately punishing those responsible for them. Holiday was simultaneously lauded for her emotional, racial and musical integrity in recording and continuing to perform 'Strange Fruit', while remaining of particular interest to the authorities for her personal frailties.

Josephson's venue, like Holiday, was of interest to the Federal Bureau of Narcotics (FBN). The FBN was aware of the singer and her drug use prior to the recording of 'Strange Fruit', but its operational ire exploded with zeal in the years following the song's release and subsequent popularity. Holiday's drug addiction (linked to a childhood dominated by neglect and sexual violence) became the target of FBN policy with undercover agents deployed to track her. Following the FBN's successful prosecution, conviction and imprisonment of Holiday in 1947, hurdles were erected to make the resumption of her career difficult. Despite this, she retained 'Strange Fruit' as her concert closer.

Contempt for the cultural and commercial power amassed by Billie Holiday – 'Lady Day' – thanks to her musical abilities was such that a photograph of her dying was needlessly issued to the media. Shrunken through addiction and yet temporarily rallying following treatment for heart and liver problems, she was pictured handcuffed to her hospital bed following her arrest, while still a patient, for drug possession. This invasive image and its dissemination served as a final power-play to sway narrative and representational authority.

Ella Fitzgerald's singing of the Great American Songbook – the canon of compositional brilliance culled from theatre, jazz and burgeoning cinema that has come to define popular entertainment in the early twentieth century – brought awareness of her talent, capabilities and charm to America. Her dual octave range, equal parts ebullience and power, could have allowed her comfortably to continue to sing with the orchestra of her mentor Chick Webb following his untimely death. However, under the guidance of manager Norman Granz, Fitzgerald took up permanent residence in the very soul of America's prescribed songbook. She followed a recording of works of George Gershwin with separate albums – the songbook series – covering classics by Cole Porter, Rodgers and Hart, the Gershwin brothers (George and Ira), Jerome Kern, Johnny Mercer and others, material that all but wallpapered American popular entertainment in the opening decades of the twentieth century.

These recordings established Fitzgerald as the 'First Lady of Song'. But she did not simply 'jazzify' the Great American Songbook (an immense enough feat): what she did was to refresh material already valued because it feels forever new. She did this while simultaneously redrawing the template of female jazz vocalization. By entering the realm of the (media-declared) sound of the nation, Fitzgerald vocally traversed boundaries formerly marking where (stylistically and physically) a Black woman could go, what she could and could not sing and with whom she could and could not perform in the 1930s and 1940s. Her songbook recordings were more than the intermingling of eras and styles. They were declarations of the extension of the scope of jazz vocal stylization; confirmation that jazz vocalization was a valid, professional, intriguing and engaging source. Fitzgerald's vocals, crystalline and buoyant, permitted her to spring up with jack-in-the-box excitability on her 1939 debut single, 'A-Tisket, A-Tasket', or to embody the yearning of 'Ev'ry Time We Say Goodbye' by Cole Porter. And yet Fitzgerald was more than this. She was also the singer capable of soaring over bands and orchestras, who recorded cherished duet albums with contemporary Louis Armstrong, who held musical court on collaborative albums and tours with beloved Counts (Basie) and Dukes (Ellington). But despite this body of work, it was her friendship with Marilyn Monroe that had to be called upon to ensure that Fitzgerald's confirmed booking at the Mocambo Club, Los Angeles, in 1955 would be fulfilled by its owners.[7]

In August the same year a 14-year-old boy from Chicago, Emmett Till, was abducted and murdered in Mississippi for offending a white woman.[8] Later that year

Ella Fitzgerald and Norman Granz in the
recording studio, late 1950s

Ella Fitzgerald and Marilyn Monroe at the
Tiffany Club, Hollywood, 1954

Fitzgerald was arrested at Houston's Music Hall in Texas (alongside trumpeter Dizzy Gillespie, fellow musicians and her assistant) for 'gambling', despite being in a separate room to the card game. Her manager, Norman Granz, was also detained after confronting police with his suspicions that the arrests related to their signed agreement with the venue not to play to a segregated audience. Their arrival at the local police station was photographed by paparazzi. The booking officer asked Fitzgerald for her autograph.

In a rare moment of candour, Fitzgerald spoke about the pressures of pleasing fans and enduring racial indignities while seeking to perform live to them; of being penalized and degraded for wanting to sing to all fans on an equal footing; and of the internal, emotional and professional conflicts this creates for Black performers seeking to please Black audiences against the ritualistic pleasure some venue owners and police officers derived from emasculating them by disrupting this exchange:

> Maybe I'm stepping out (of line), but I have to say it, because it's in my heart. It makes you feel bad to think we can't go down through certain parts of the South and give a concert like we can overseas and have everybody just come to hear the music and enjoy the music because of the prejudice thing that's going on.

> I used to always clam up because you (hear people) say, 'Oh, gee, show people should stay out of politics.' But we have travelled so much and been embarrassed so much. (Fans) can't understand why you don't play in Alabama, or (ask), 'Why can't you have a concert?'[9]

A piano-playing child prodigy, Nina Simone dreamed of becoming the first African American classical pianist to headline Carnegie Hall solo. She realized her dream – in part – in 1961, in concerts alongside Miriam Makeba, and Sonny Rollins, John Coltrane and Thelonious Monk, and went on to fulfil her ambition of headlining Carnegie Hall solo in 1963. But by that time her musical and personal convictions demanded that she express herself beyond the classical music of her childhood. Simone felt compelled to confront through her art the lethal racial violence and large-scale public protests that were rampant and widespread. However, married to and managed by her husband, Andrew

Stroud, Simone was advised not to court controversy and 'ruin' opportunities invited by her dedicated talent by focusing on 'the racial issue'. But race-driven public murders were as callous as they were flagrant: a teenage boy tortured and killed by two men for acts later retracted by his accuser; the NAACP's Field Secretary, Medger Evers, shot dead outside his home in Jackson, Mississippi, hours after President Kennedy's live national civil rights address.[10]

And so the accomplishment of Simone's dream in 1963 was soon eclipsed. We know this because she wrote 'Mississippi Goddam' that year, in tribute to Evers and as a response to the shocking bombing of a church in which four schoolgirls – the youngest just 11 years old – were killed in Birmingham, Alabama. Martin Luther King Jr had delivered his 'I Have a Dream' speech at the celebrated March on Washington for Jobs and Freedom just the month before the children's murders.[11]

In 'Mississippi Goddam' Simone's horror at the rising tally of dead is spliced with frustration and disgust at the social mobilization of racism that also kills the spirit and suppresses the quality of life in the living. The song encapsulates psychological befuddlement and belly-deep rage at the nation's willingness to permit regional orgies of lethal race-driven violence. Over her galloping piano strokes Simone unapologetically curses (albeit by standards of the 1960s), the song's title laying bare the absurd tropes that seek to justify the continuance of racism. Thus she shames its beneficiaries.

To craft protest music, to create freedom songs of such singular and collective might, to continually perform them while the landscape refused to respond at pace contributed to Simone's disillusionment – disillusionment that she also put into song. Whether updating 'Mississippi Goddam' in the coming years to reference new killings, new marches, new sorrows, or delivering the scathing 'Old Jim Crow', the funereal 'I Wish I Knew How it Would Feel to Be Free' or the invective 'Backlash Blues', the pace of change (like the introduction of the 1964 Voting Rights Act) was slower than the intimidation and violence that sought to stop it.

Simone developed friendships with the upper echelon of Black rights representatives (she and her family were neighbours of Malcolm X, his wife, Dr Betty Shabazz, and their daughters); Luther King Jr became a friend; Harlem

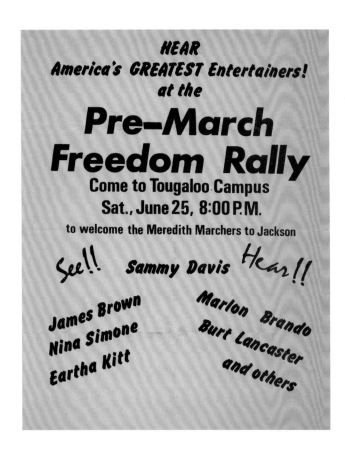

Renaissance alumni were confidants and collaborators (indeed, 'Backlash Blues' evolved from a poem written by renowned playwright and author Langston Hughes). Their direct knowledge of issues and political policies informed Simone's lyrics and complemented her instrumental versatility. When she recorded covers ('Ain't Got No/I Got Life' and Holiday's 'Strange Fruit') they radiated with her authority.

In due, tragic course Simone would be robbed of these friendships through assassination or terminal illnesses. 'To Be Young, Gifted and Black', her tribute to her best friend, playwright Lorraine Hansberry, is a love baton pass: its title taken from Hansberry's play of the same name. The song celebrates Hansberry, her work and its impact, while also, through its nursery-rhyme style arrangement, uplifting impressionable younger listeners who have been misled by society into believing the opposite of its title. Within days of the assassination of Martin Luther King Jr, Simone had written and was performing the resigned, embittered and despondent 'Why? (The King of Love is Dead)'. Delicate in its sorrow, instrumental space was given for Simone to intone that he was '... always living with the threat of death ahead' and here, now, the '... king of love is dead'.

Too little acknowledgement is given to the toll that repeatedly performing such material imparts on its creator/performer, the emotional tax of crafting material concurrent to the violence it speaks of and then, for years – decades – afterwards replaying the rage and pain. The virulence of racism and the slow pace of change affected Simone, steering decisions such as her non-payment of taxes and emigration from the United States. While it would be years before an undiagnosed mental health condition granted understanding of her outlook and behaviour, her music was listened to but Simone herself not often heeded. She would become classed as 'difficult', 'moody'. A 'diva'.

Aretha Franklin, like Simone, Holiday and Fitzgerald, was musically adept at seizing the creative challenge and

Flier for a pre-march freedom rally for the Meredith Marchers who aimed to promote black voter registration and defy racism, 1966
Collection of the Smithsonian National Museum of African American History and Culture, Gift from the Trumpauer-Mulholland Collection

Sleeve for Nina Simone's single 'Mississippi Goddam/Sealion Woman', 1964
Collection of the Smithsonian National Museum of African American History and Culture

Nina Simone performing at Ronnie Scott's, London, 9 January 1984. Photograph by David Corio

Aretha Franklin performing at the
Hammersmith Odeon, London, May 1968

FBI poster for the arrest of activist Angela
Davis, 1970
Collection of the Smithsonian National
Museum of African American History and
Culture

commercial value of reinterpreting popular songs. Her
stabbing march through Otis Redding's original recording
of 'Respect' made it an anthem by 1967, as much for its
demand for consideration and mutual respect within a
relationship as serving as both a treaty for feminism and a
rallying cry for racial equality. Aretha's cover of Simone's 'To
Be Young, Gifted and Black' for her highly rated album of
the same name also contained 'Border Song (Holy Moses)',
her interpretation of Elton John's 'Border Song'. Both
interpretations unite elements that are evident throughout
Aretha's original material and her astonishing body of
wider recorded output: her expressive, propulsive piano
playing and soaring, powerful and, ultimately, enriching
vocalization.

Like Nina Simone, Aretha Franklin came to count
Martin Luther King Jr as a friend (alongside the top tier
of American gospel artists – Clara Ward, Mahalia Jackson,
James Cleveland and Sam Cooke). Franklin, too, was
managed by her first husband, Ted White (who was
also billed as songwriter and co-producer on landmark
recordings for the Atlantic Records label until their bitter
divorce in 1969). White, like Stroud, preferred his wife to
relegate her commitment to King's requests, to which she
responded that she would 'always' support him. Many
celebrities, like managers Stroud and White, understood the
reputational risks that unjustly penalized Black celebrities for
participating in the civil rights struggle. They also knew of
the risks of simply *being* a Black celebrity in America.

The tableau of organizations serving to promote and
protect racial and social rights – the Southern Christian
Leadership Conference (SCLC) founded by Martin
Luther King Jr, Pan Africanism, the Nation of Islam and
the Black Panther Party – offered different paths to the
same destination. When Angela Davis, former professor
at the University of California (UCLA), Los Angeles, and
former member of the Student Nonviolent Coordinating
Committee (SNCC),[12] the Black Panther and Communist
parties, was declared America's most wanted woman by
the FBI in 1970 (following the use of guns registered in her
name in the killing of a judge and others during a court
stand-off), Aretha Franklin offered to stand her bail after
she was captured and charged. Franklin issued a press
statement confirming the offer (more than $1 million in
today's money):

Aretha Franklin receiving an award from
Martin Luther King, Detroit, 1967
UM Bentley Library. C.L. Franklin Papers

Aretha Franklin performs at the White House
for Barack Obama's inauguration as US
President, Washington, DC, 2009

*My daddy says I don't know what I'm doing. Well, I respect him, of course, but I'm going to stick by my beliefs. Angela Davis must go free. Black people will be free. I've been locked up (for disturbing the peace in Detroit) and I know you got to disturb the peace when you can't get no peace. Jail is hell to be in. I'm going to see her free if there is any justice in our courts, not because I believe in Communism, but because she's a Black woman and she wants freedom for Black people. I have the money; I got it from Black people – they made me financially able to have it – and I want to use it in ways to help people.*[13]

Franklin's offer was never taken up, and Davis was eventually cleared of all charges. The two never met. But Franklin's public stance spoke of the breadth of her philanthropic convictions, her conscience and her willingness to overcome the opposition encouraged by the media in the public's perception of African American civil rights organizations (some more 'respectable', 'safer' or 'good for America' than others). Franklin, the stature of her reputation based on the stature of her voice, remained a broad bridge upon which to rely. How else to explain, following her work with and for activists throughout the 1950s and 1960s, that it would be the Queen of Soul who would be called upon to sing at the Democratic National Convention in Chicago, four months after the assassination of Martin Luther King Jr and at the inaugurations of three Democrat presidents (Carter,[14] Clinton and Obama) in the decades that followed? Far from simply a top-tier booking, Franklin was the physical and sonic embodiment of the African American musical journey of pain over circumstance: the music, from gospel to soul, that accompanies the lived experience of living as an African American in a society that had enslaved your ancestors and denied a variety of social rights on the basis of being Black. Lauded, endorsed and commercially popular, Franklin faced public expectations away from the microphone and piano. When she didn't fulfil these – from minor deviations like taking her handbag *everywhere* (red carpet or on stage) to not being drawn into discussions about the vocal capabilities of younger singers or remaining resolutely private about becoming a mother at the ages of 12 and 16 – in due course her reluctance or remoteness in relation to subjects she deemed off-limits rendered her 'difficult'. Over time Franklin communicated less with the press, which allowed the imposed assertions to stick: 'unrivalled talent of her age' didn't have the same ring as 'superstar diva'.

Although it was American jazz that inspired South African singer and songwriter Miriam Makeba and advanced her international musical career, she retained her focus on African politics and activism. Miriam was 16 years old when apartheid was introduced in South Africa in 1948, just three years after the end of the Second World War. Reversing the implementation of white supremacism in every realm of life, which had marked the Black majority as an 'inferior' minority without equal rights, was a cause for which Makeba fought until the official end of apartheid in 1994. Her voice, musical and spoken, was her weapon.

Makeba began her music career with The Manhattan Brothers, the popular South African Jazz vocal quartet who melded traditional Zulu mbube music into their performative framework. Over three decades the Manhattan Brothers' musicality attracted leading talents to their line-up, including celebrated trumpeter (and Makeba's second husband) Hugh Masekela and jazz musician Josef Gwangwa. It was not unusual for members of the group to perform in touring musicals, and it was while out of the country promoting a film, *Come Back, Africa*, in 1959 that Makeba met US singer Harry Belafonte. Their collaborative relationship went on to span an impressive musical output: international tours, Grammy award-winning albums and a new approach to the performative examination and celebration of identity. Belafonte's Jamaican-American and Makeba's Xhosa origins led them both on expansive journeys through folk musicality. For Makeba this was crystallized in the international success of 'Qongqothwane (The Click Song)' and, significantly, 'Pata Pata', which deliberately spoke against the apartheid system in English and Xhosa, using layered vocal harmonies and ululations.

Makeba's musical and cultural pride – always sartorially evident and linguistically identifiable – led to an invitation to speak at the United Nations Special Commission on Apartheid. Reading from a prepared statement (overleaf), she called for a boycott of her home country in order to advance change of the apartheid regime then nearing its second decade. Her speech, from which the following extract is taken, was delivered on 16 July 1963:

*South Africa is a world problem and the burning question of the day. One which all people of goodwill the world over must participate in finding a solution.*

*... I have already stated that you and the Committee know that the political situation is tense ... this, therefore, did not leave us with any option but to ask the United Nations to take positive action against the South African government. By positive action I mean, of course, that the United Nations should put into action the very good resolutions calling for a complete boycott on South Africa and especially the sending of arms by outside powers to South Africa. I have not the slightest doubt that these arms will be used against the African women and children ... I appeal with all the strength I can muster that the United Nations and the entire world should do their utmost to compel the Verwoerd[15] government to open the doors and prisons and concentration camps in South Africa.*

*... On the admission of the South African government some five thousand people have in recent months been put behind prison bars ... My country has been turned by the Verwoerd government into a huge prison ... I feel certain that the time has come for the whole of humanity to shout 'halt!' And to act with firmness to stop these crazy rulers from dragging our country into a horrifying disaster.[16]*

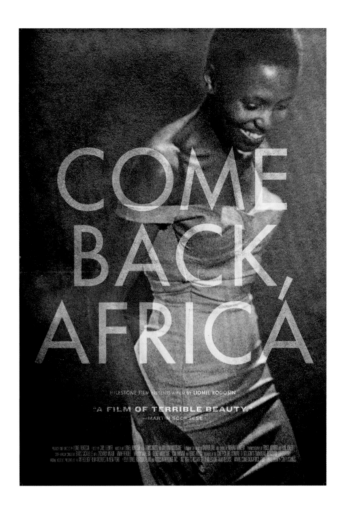

Makeba spoke of the 1960 Sharpeville massacre, in which 69 Black people were killed by armed police during an anti-apartheid march organized by the Pan Africanist Congress[17] and the African National Congress.[18] She identified Nelson Mandela among the names of 5,000 people held in detention.

The South African authorities, in response to her pointed UN address, censored Makeba's music from national radio and revoked her citizenship (she had been barred from entry to the country three years earlier, on arrival for her mother's funeral). Mama Africa, the 'Empress of African Song', was thus made stateless by the apartheid government.

Makeba's activism continued and in 1968 she married Stokely Carmichael, a former SNCC chairman and freedom

Miriam Makeba on the poster for the 2012 re-release of *Come Back, Africa* (1959)

Miriam Makeba giving her speech at
the Special Committee on the Policies
of Apartheid of the Government of the
Republic of South Africa, 16 July 1963

rider).[19] Carmichael (who later changed his name to Kwame Ture) had popularized the term 'Black Power' and designed a logo that would later be adopted by the Black Panther Party (BPP). In 1969 the FBI declared the BPP a 'Communist organization' and 'enemy of the US government'. Their marriage had a negative impact on Makeba's commercial success in the USA and the couple went to live in Guinea. When their marriage ended in 1979, Makeba found that she was the primary South African singer sought for international tours and collaborations. But it would take Nelson Mandela, former head of the ANC and prisoner of the South African government for 27 years, to coax her to return home following his release from prison in 1990. And return she did, after 31 years of forced exile, later becoming South Africa's UN Goodwill Ambassador.

The media's integral role in the dissemination of popular entertainment has ensured that the word 'diva' is an established global term. It is also a malleable one, with its meaning, complimentary or accusatory in intent, capable of exalting the subject or imparting a negative reputational slur. As this book demonstrates, the opening and closing decades of the twentieth century have shown how wildly 'diva' can oscillate between the positive and the damning, all the while remaining steadfastly gendered – a pointed reference of and to *she* who dares to possess artistry that appeals.

And yet for Billie Holiday, Ella Fitzgerald, Nina Simone, Aretha Franklin and Miriam Makeba, 'diva' was not the foremost challenge to be faced or surmounted in the professionalization of their musical talents. Their respective battles – which the passage of time allows us to look upon individually *and* collectively – demonstrated that their musical successes and reputational authorities weren't concerned with confronting that word. If anything, 'diva' was a bridesmaid in the wedding party of their concern. Race and gender – socialized into racism and sexism – were the pre-eminent, twinned evils they faced. These artists first had to assail the social and political confines imposed upon them as a result of their race and gender. The behavioural politics 'diva' has contemporaneously come to define and impart pulled up at the rear of their battles.

There IS a triumph to be observed in having 'diva' attracting shorter shrift – even if its relegation was due to the behemoths of racism and sexism.

By dint of birth and the social histories of their respective times, these Black female artists had to battle for the right to be heard, seen and succeed musically on equal par with their male (Black or white) and female (white) peers against the structural and institutional confines of racism and sexism. For them all to have incorporated oppositional response to these forces *into* their music, the performance *of* their music, and to bring oppositional responses to media, state organizations, the music industry and governments were power plays of expressed bravery that stand beyond the expectations of an entertainer's duties. As such, a battle was won here: over the power of 'diva' to constrict. 'Diva', like racism and sexism, was not granted permission to invade, limit or define their artistry. A victory – of sorts – was attained.

# Rule the World:
# Status, Power, Freedom

Veronica Castro

Dolly Parton poses in front of an image of herself holding a Dolly doll. Photograph by Craig McDean, 2020. Background photograph by Hope Powell

Dolly Parton at the opening of Dollywood,
1986

**There's something so special about a woman who dominates in a man's world. It takes a certain grace, strength, intelligence, fearlessness, and the nerve to never take no for an answer.[1]**

Where you find a diva, you'll likely find a businessperson, a self-starter, a hustler: extending her creativity and occupying space in the overwhelmingly male worlds of the music and movie industries. Female entertainers of the late nineteenth century were among the first businesswomen, having agency at a time when professional involvement by those of the 'fairer sex' was frowned upon, if not prohibited outright. Divas have always been able to use the fruits of their talents as a means of escape, from a life of limited opportunity and expectations or to an alternate reality where their choices are their own. Their power lies in the freedom to choose.

We meet our contemporary divas in a world that in many ways is much better equipped to receive them than ever. We are in the midst of a boom of cultural hashtag slogans for female success: #LeanIn, #GirlBoss, #BossBitch, etc. are all calls for female empowerment, achieved, so the thinking goes, by adopting typically 'masculine' practices while asserting the freedom to represent and express yourself in whatever way you choose. While divas of the past would have been allowed to display their wealth, it was frowned upon to display the manners or language of their male counterparts in polite society; today it can all be done in public and out loud. Even the word 'diva' itself has now been added to the lexicon as a term relating to female empowerment, success and entrepreneurial spirit.

With their outrageous amounts of talent, vision, hard work and sheer *moxie*, some of those divas from the last 70 years who have taken their destinies by the scruff of the neck, pushing past what's expected to forge a new future for themselves, and consequently those that follow, are celebrated here. These divas have been able to channel their success into something larger than themselves, their sound or their voices.

Dolly Parton's journey might well be the definition of a rags to riches story. Born and raised in a one-room cabin in Tennessee and the fourth of 12 children, she was playing guitar by the age of six. Signing a recording contract at 19, she released her first country single, *Dumb Blonde*, in 1966. Her star continued to rise, setting the stage for a pop-pivot

in the mid-1970s, which introduced her to a whole new audience. In 1980 she starred in the comedy film *9 to 5*, securing her an Oscar nomination and sending her fame into orbit.

Parton is a songteller[2] – combining the threads of a rich Southern oral tradition, a Pentecostal Christian upbringing and the pathos, tenderness and humour wrought from her childhood experiences to weave into songs that appeal to a mass audience beyond the traditional country music market. In interviews and in performance she is disarmingly charming, self-deprecating. Above all she is a songwriter: a creative powerhouse whose songs have been covered and sampled endlessly across genres and generations. A self-styled 'Backwoods Barbie', she sings about the hardship and realities of a woman's 'down-home' life while looking like a pop-art version of 'exaggerated womanhood'.[3] Her image worked for sales but led to frustration behind the scenes. Nashville and country music were and generally remain hotbeds of traditional conservative values – a 'good woman's' place was rarely on stage, and never in the boardroom. 'Dumb Blonde' seemed to be the broad perception of her within the music business, and Parton's experience of the music industry was one of underestimation and diminution: the age-old questioning of the legitimacy and authenticity of a woman's art and business nous based on her manner, her look. The broadsides came from women as well as men. A notorious 1977 interview by Barbara Walters questioned whether Parton worried about others thinking she was a joke due to the way she looked:

> *People have thought the joke was on me but it's actually been on the public. I know exactly what I'm doing and I can change it any time ... I am sure of myself as a person, I'm sure of my talent...*[4]

Like Marilyn Monroe before her, Parton utilized this blonde bombshell persona to infiltrate spaces of male power, making some prudent decisions along the way,[5] starting her own publishing company at 20 and retaining publishing

rights to the vast majority of her songs. In 1986 she became the co-owner of Dollywood (p. 106), a theme park tribute to her persona and her values, a chance for fans to physically walk through her story. It is also the ultimate pay-back to the land and communities that formed and continue to inspire her. Parton's ambition was never purely rooted in career success (although escaping poverty was a driver) but by a guiding principle of service. She believes that her talents are God-given and her duty is to put them to use for good:

> I feel like I touch people, I feel like I make a difference, I feel like I can write songs for people who can't express themselves.[6]

Self-expression was never a challenge for Barbra Streisand, the plucky all-rounder with an almost incomparable tick-list of talent – all-singing, dancing, acting AND directing, Streisand is the complete Hollywood package, albeit with a working-class Brooklyn accent. Her rise to global stardom took the well-trodden diva route via nightclub and theatre stages. By 1964, aged just 21, she had signed her first recording contract with Columbia Records. The contract stipulated that in return for a lesser fee, Streisand would retain full artistic control of her songs and output. These were unshakeable ground rules that would define the rest of her (so-far) six-decade career: remaining true to one's artistic vision, remaining authentically oneself and never accepting less than you think you are worth. Those who knew her in her early career describe Streisand as an unstoppable force, a juggernaut with a course set to inevitable stardom. She had what so many other artists lack: an unwavering self-possession and belief in her own talents and potential.

Streisand's major career break was landing the part of Fanny Brice in *Funny Girl* on Broadway in 1964. As a vehicle for showcasing her multiple talents, the role of Fanny was

a gift, seemingly purpose-built for Streisand: memorable songs[7] to highlight her soaring, bright vocals and a script that enhanced her playfulness and comedic timing, but which also allowed for her tenderness and sensitivity to shine. Streisand went on to star in the movie adaptation (her debut movie role), resulting in her first Academy Award win, in 1968.

Winning an Oscar went some way to legitimizing Streisand's place in what was still very much the 'old boys' club' of the Hollywood system. Further successful films followed, but it wasn't until 1983 with *Yentl* that Streisand would make history (overleaf). Despite her proven success, she had to fight for over a decade to get the film made: she was too inexperienced, too young, too *female*. *Yentl* saw Streisand become the first woman to star in, write, produce and direct her own movie. She won the Golden Globe for best director that year but didn't even receive a nomination for the same category at the Oscars, allegedly due to her 'aggression':

> That word 'aggressive' ... We're just measured by a different standard. He's 'committed.' She's 'obsessed.' It's been said that a man's reach should exceed his grasp. Why can't that be true of a woman?[8]

Until 2020 Streisand remained the only woman to receive a Golden Globe Best Director award.

Then there was the issue of her looks. She was repeatedly asked to 'consider' cosmetic surgery on a nose that was too 'ethnic' and therefore did not fit the look of a bankable leading lady. Streisand refused – staunch in her resolution to not assimilate or fall prey to the whim of the 1960s All-American beauty standard: sweet, dainty, picture-perfect. She embodied a new, revolutionary image of sexuality that welcomed those who had so far been kept out of the room, kicking open the doors for alternative representations of femininity in the mainstream.

Visibility matters; but how to fight for representation when you're concealed by design? Lata Mangeshkar (1929–2022) was India's leading Bollywood playback singer – during an 80-year career her recorded vocals would accompany the actions of the heroines of the Bollywood screen. She was beloved in her home nation, known as the 'Nightingale of India' – the soundtrack to decades of

Barbra Streisand receiving her Academy Award for Best Actress in a Leading Role for *Funny Girl*, 1968

Lata Mangeshkar poses during the launch
of the 'Humsafar' 2013 calendar in Mumbai,
2012

Left:
Barbra Streisand behind the camera during
the filming of *Yentl*, 1983

star-crossed lovers and family feuds on screen. She would
provide the raw emotion, the subtle inflections, the lyrical
flourishes while the invariably young and beautiful actor on
screen would emote the action of the scene.

Mangeshkar actually began her career on screen but
soon realized that she preferred singing to acting. Her big
break came recording the song 'Aayega Aanewala' for the
film *Mahal*. Her voice made such an impact that she was
credited publicly, almost unheard of in an industry where
playback singers were expected to be heard but not
seen. Her success had inadvertently sparked a revolution
in the playback world – the voices that drove the movies
that supported the industry as a whole would now be
recognized in their own right. She also 'initiated the
conversation about royalties for playback singers',[9] insisting
that they were given due royalty payments. Like Edith Piaf
(1915-1963) in France, Mangeshkar shouldered the honour
of being the voice of her nation. Part of the cultural identity
of India, she was arguably the most influential Indian singer
in popular memory. In 2001 she was awarded India's highest
civilian award, the Bharat Ratna. She will be remembered for
progressing the cause of the hitherto hidden female artists
in Bollywood.

Some divas understand the power of hiding, of
withholding a 'little something'. Adele's appeal sits very
much in the camp of the unpretentious and the authentic,
with sweeping, cathartic songs that manage to bridge jazz
and soul styles with the outlook, beats and awareness of
popular music *now*. By bypassing trends and aiming straight
for the heartstrings, Adele's music has the power to connect
to a listener on an emotional level directly. Her appeal
lies not only in the music but in her persona: disarmingly
relatable, with a manner that wasn't media-trained to within
an inch of its life but that has enough spice, charm and
humour to keep us hooked. Adele is a woman both very
much of her time and defiantly outside of it – among her
biggest musical influences, Ella Fitzgerald and Etta James sit
alongside Björk and The Spice Girls. Adele does not fit the
mould for the modern pop diva – neither figuratively nor
literally (perhaps predictably a lot – too much – has been
written on her size and weight) – she is humble yet brash
and resolutely British in her banter.

Adele's power now may be explained by the origins of
her career as a recording artist. Her career began when she

Adele holds her Grammy Awards for Best
Female Pop Vocal Performance and Best
New Artist at the 51st annual Grammy
Awards, Los Angeles, 2009

signed to British independent label XL Recordings aged 18. This contract allowed her the time and space to build on the songwriting voice she had begun to establish, without the pressures of major label or media expectations. By the time her XL deal expired in 2016, Adele had built a formula that was hard to argue with – the sound she had created and cultivated on her own terms with albums *19*, *21* and *25* were phenomenal global successes, and she had the exponentially growing audience and sales numbers to prove it. As a device, the simple economics of increasing demand by decreasing supply – laying low between releases – worked to satisfy both her artistic needs and the financial demands of the business. Adele was following in the lineage of divas who have drawn power from their ability to simply withdraw from the all-seeing public eye – stars such as Sade and Kate Bush – whose careers not only survived their absence but in most cases were boosted, and who crucially had the autonomy to take these periods of retreat. She put it like this following the release of her single 'Hello' (2015), her return after a three-year hiatus: 'I'm just going to sing now because I want to, and I'll make records when I want to and not because someone is forcing me to do it ... I'd fire them if they tried!'[10]

Her $90 million move to Sony Music in 2016 was the biggest record deal for a British recording artist ever. Adele's astronomical rise has been unique among her peers, eschewing the trappings of contemporary pop artists, sidestepping endorsement contracts, product placement in music videos and movie roles, and without a significant social media presence. In fact in this sense one could argue that she is peer*less*. One thing remains the same: Adele is not writing on demand. She writes because she must:

> I don't think there's any expectation of sincerity left in music for artists ... and I think to be an artist ... it comes from deep within us and it's a necessity that we have to put it [the music] out ... It's just a transaction now ... that's not why I got into music.[11]

Janet Jackson was *born* into music. Before arriving at her current diva form, Jackson had to survive the various stages of her initiation. A child TV star in the shadow of her wildly successful brothers (The Jackson Five), she was occasionally made to join them in appearances as the token cutie-pie female sibling. The transition to solo stardom was complicated. Asserting independence, finding one's own voice and point of view when you've been sold as part of a package wasn't easy. By the release of her third album, *Control*, in 1986, she was primed and ready.

The album packed a mighty punch, signalling Jackson embracing autonomy over her career, image and musical direction. Her presentation was powerful, with utilitarian, militaristic outfits that were more a call to arms than a celebration of sexuality. Its impact was substantial: sales, awards and accolades followed but it was in its influence that its impact was really felt. Musically it was an experimental mixture of pop, R&B and rap that hitherto had not been heard in mainstream pop. Significantly, Janet was a Black woman operating on her own terms. A role model for Black girls – a contemporary of Madonna but crucially a visible and proud African American woman who spoke to Black pride, liberation, frank sexuality and female independence (p. 114).

*Janet Jackson's Rhythm Nation 1814* followed in 1989, this time a more pointedly politically charged album whose lyrics were socially conscious, tackling topical issues including social inequality, racism and substance abuse. Combined with her precision choreography, her music and performance style have inspired every dancing diva since and has set the industry standard for the contemporary pop concert experience, not to mention the modern music video. The album saw her receive a Best Producer Grammy nomination, the first woman ever to be recognized as such.

At the 1997 Soul Train music awards Jackson received the Lena Horne Career Achievement award from Maya Angelou. During her acceptance speech she acknowledged her undeniable place in the diva legacy timeline:

> Recently I wrote a song entitled 'Can't be Stopped'. The message I wanted to communicate is this: You can go anywhere you want to, as long as you don't forget where you come from. I will always remember where I come from, and whose shoulders I stand upon.

The pop divas who stand on *her* shoulders are now some of the biggest stars on the planet.

Beyoncé was already impossibly famous by the time

she officially went solo. Spending her youth and early adulthood in Destiny's Child, one of the most successful female groups of all time, had seasoned her for fame and furnished her with a ready-made fanbase who were ready to hear more. But perhaps not even she could have predicted what would follow. Embracing the loaded freedom of being a solo performer, Beyoncé was faced with the possibilities available to you when you're beholden to no one but yourself: 'I just wanted people to really hear me, hear my voice and my tastes. For the first time, I wasn't afraid, I didn't feel limited'.[12]

An enigmatic superstar, all we know about Beyoncé are the things she is willing to share, and this precious intel is delivered as and when, and is devoured hungrily by the press and an ever-attentive army of fans, the 'Beyhive'. This approach extends to her music and Beyoncé has cemented her status as queen of the surprise 'drop'.

The release of Beyoncé's *Lemonade* in 2016 revolutionized the contemporary pop landscape. This visual album, a first, wove music videos into a narrative film that not only sounded great but was visually accomplished and breathed fresh life into the album format in a world of streaming and on-demand content. *Lemonade* is a tribute to independence, Black history, her own Southern heritage and a reflection on the current political and social climate, as seen through the lens of an African American woman. The lyrics championed self-empowerment, often subverting masculine/feminine relationship tropes, with Beyoncé recast as the benevolent breadwinner and arbiter of worth in the partnership (overleaf).

We know Beyoncé best, perhaps, through her performance persona Sasha Fierce. Sasha embodied the full freedoms that Beyoncé *off* stage keeps hidden. The spirit of Sasha was in full effect for Beyoncé's performance at the 2018 Coachella, Valley Music and Arts Festival in California, perhaps the ultimate expression of the diva performance (p. 117). This was an unabashed demonstration of creativity, energy and exuberance; an

audacious thunderclap of power and prowess. To be in the audience of a Beyoncé show is also to experience the palpable energy of the Beyhive – the auditorium is a site of pilgrimage, the hive is enriched and empowered by a vision of its idol.

Beyoncé sings the gospel of self-empowerment to her fans, of being an active participant in your own life, of overcoming your insecurities and circumstances to achieve greatness. She tells her fans to make lemonade when life gives you lemons, and they listen. In 2022 this messaging has been reworked in a paean to the possibilities of ecstatic joy, freedom of expression and communal experience with the release of her seventh solo album, *Renaissance*. Following the album, a remix of the first single, 'Break my Soul', was released – this time a diva collaboration extraordinaire with Madonna, reworking the single with Madonna's 1990 hit, 'Vogue'. In it Beyoncé recasts Madonna's original who's who list of Old Hollywood legends as Black music pioneers and rising stars – a shout out to her influences and influencees, reframing a modern pop classic as a tribute to the music that made her, and the music made *from* her.

Alongside her husband, Jay-Z, Beyoncé is one half of a billionaire music power couple. Through her charity BeyGOOD she has donated millions to humanitarian causes and has been a vocal advocate for social justice, political and environmental issues.[13] As far as endorsements go, even former US president Barack Obama said that Beyoncé 'could not be a better role model for my girls'.[14] Speaking on her responsibility to her *own* offspring, she said this:

> It's important to me that they [her daughters] see themselves as CEOs, as bosses, and that they know they can write the script for their own lives – that they can speak their minds and they have no ceiling.[15]

Rihanna is second only to Madonna in the ranks of biggest selling female performers of all time and was recently certified as the music world's first solo female billionaire. How did a 'little seed, from an island far away'[16] rise to the top of diva mountain? Auditioning for Def Jam Recordings in 2005, it was clear that she had 'the stuff', that she added something that only a select few have. As Jay-Z recalls, 'You see someone who comes in and you know if

---

Janet Jackson at the Diamond Pop Awards in Antwerp, Belgium, 1989

Stills from Beyoncé's 'Formation' from her 'visual album' *Lemonade*, 2016

Beyoncé performs at the Coachella Festival, Indio, California, 2018

they have that look about them, that star quality – you can't deny it'.[17] Eight albums in and Rihanna has cemented herself as one of the major power players in the music industry, regardless of gender. As one of the superstars of the new digital age, Rihanna has taken the Madonna blueprint – openness to change and a commitment to outspoken authenticity, collaboration and provocation – and reworked it for the twenty-first century, reshaping it in her own style. However, as a non-American, Black performer, Rihanna was not setting off from the same starting block.

Like Madonna, Rihanna's sense of chameleonic reinvention, of the now and the next, infuses her creative output. Flitting between genres and styles, her unpredictability has kept her relevant and at the forefront of the modern pop music zeitgeist. She is hard to pin down, whether musically or aesthetically: a freedom to explore and a rule against repetition guides her process and aligns with her branding. She trademarked her surname, Fenty, in 2014 and launched the first company bearing the name, Fenty Beauty, in 2017. As CEO, Rihanna kick-started a revolution of accessibility within the cosmetics industry, creating a line of foundation shades that catered to the historically under-served people of colour who were used to the bare minimum from most other established brands. She has since added lingerie (Savage x Fenty) and skincare (Fenty Skin) businesses to her empire. Rihanna walked the walk when it came to diversity and inclusion, challenging notions of what constitutes a model body, a sexy body, a body worth adorning or desiring.

The diva using their image for branding is not a new concept. Josephine Baker capitalized on the sensation of her defining 'Eton crop' hairstyle by putting her name to a line of hair products; silent movie star Mary Pickford released a line of branded cosmetics; and Hollywood icon Elizabeth Taylor kicked off the now familiar notion of the lucrative celebrity-scent franchise with the 1985 release of her fragrance, 'Passion'. These products were extensions of their personalities, a way for fans to align themselves with greatness, with something bigger than themselves. Fenty products allow fans to experience a little of the essence of Rihanna, to buy in to their idol.

Rihanna's empire is a means to an end, not the goal itself:

*My money is not for me; it's always the thought that I can help someone else … The world can really make you believe that the wrong things are priority, and it makes you really miss the core of life, what it means to be alive.*[18]

In 2007 she was given the Harvard for Humanitarian of the Year Award. To add to her list of remarkable accomplishments she was declared a National Hero of her home nation, Barbados, on the first day of its independence in 2021 (p. 120). As the Right Excellent Rihanna, her appeal lies largely in the relatability of her persona. She embodies what playwright Jeremy O. Harris calls a 'casual immensity',[19] possessing an irresistible magnetism, an insouciant sexiness that does not pander to the male gaze; she is irreverent, wry, a little bit chaotic but together enough to be at the helm of a billion-dollar empire. Her fan interactions are legendary – she does not shy away from direct contact with 'the Navy' (her fandom) and they live for these moments of being noticed, honoured by their most high leader. The famously intense 'Navy' are among the fiercest and most committed of all the diva fandoms, brought together and galvanized by social media, with a captain in Rihanna and a family in each other.

Beyond the deals, the contracts and the empires we are left with voices – divas using them to entertain, to inspire, to provoke conversation, to move culture forward, to create communities. Divas don't just create art, they create contemporary culture. These individuals have made an impact that has gone beyond music and directly impacts lives – driving social change and acting as beacons of potential. A diva is a solo performer who stands on the shoulders of giants – who builds on the victories of the fights of their forebears, leaving in their wake new possibilities for the divas that follow. As Jay-Z said of Rihanna, 'What took me 15 or 20 years to get has taken her 10, and will take the next person 5 years. It's great to be able to help fight that fight.'[20] Perhaps the truest measure of their success will be their cultural impact, their legacy and the mark they leave on the generations to come.

Rihanna celebrates the introduction of Fenty
Beauty's range to the Ulta chain of beauty
stores, Los Angeles, March 2022

Rihanna, Barbados's 11th National Hero, at the National Honors ceremony, Bridgetown, Barbados, November 2021

Rihanna, wearing ruched chap boots created by Giuseppe Zanotti, performs on her ANTI World Tour, at San Siro Stadium, Milan, 2016

# Express Yourself: Rebel Reinvention

Lucy O'Brien

'To everyone who gave me hell and said I could not ... your resistance made me stronger ... made me the woman that I am today', Madonna said in 2016 when accepting her Billboard Woman of the Year Award.[1] Continually inventive and setting out to shock, enthral and engage, she – along with other divas in this chapter such as Lady Gaga, Björk, Lauryn Hill and Billie Eilish – has worked creatively with people's resistance, exploding the notion of what a diva should look or sound like. Through the concept of rebellion and reinvention, this chapter considers how disruptive divas have stretched the limits of genre and style. Did the negatively weighted use of the phrase 'being a diva' materialize across the twentieth century because creative women pursuing a singular vision found a way to express what they wanted? Artists like Madonna and Lady Gaga construct categories of their own, working and re-working the boundaries of popular music.

To consider what these divas have achieved, it's important to look at antecedents and the landscape for pop women in the 1960s and '70s. Creativity is a process strategically managed by the music industry. Although music genres are not static, record labels like to have marketable visual and musical codes and this leads to a reduction in risk-taking. As musicologist Keith Negus wrote, there is a tendency in record companies to 'build walls within which creativity can be contained'.[2] This process militates against female creative expression because women artists on average sell less than men and can be seen as a risky investment.[3] And if a major label artist is genre-hopping or misbehaving – or 'being a diva' – it makes her harder to sell. This chapter focuses on how key rebel divas managed to navigate through music industry networks that privileged white male cultural work, to create their own visual and musical codes.

One of the first women to make inroads into psychedelic blues rock was Janis Joplin (1943–1970), an unorthodox presence at the centre of the Haight-Ashbury scene in San Francisco. A major influence on early heavy metal screamers like Robert Plant, she mined 1920s blues for inspiration, and in particular vaudeville blues mama Bessie Smith (1894–1937). Born in Texas, Joplin began singing folk songs in coffee houses in Houston and Austin, before moving to San Francisco in 1963 and developing her searing rock style with Big Brother and the

Holding Company. She defied conventions of the racially segregated South by performing unfettered blues, usually considered an African American musical form. She also rejected the Bible Belt mores of the area where she grew up, being openly bisexual – as Jana Evans Braziel argues, 'experimental Joplin creat[ed] her own personal sexual revolution'.[4]

Much has been made of Joplin's chaotic lifestyle and capacity for excess, but she was also a dedicated performer and professional, re-working blues idioms through a number of bands, until with the Full Tilt Boogie Band she reached the magical intensity of her final album, *Pearl*, released posthumously in 1970 after she died of a heroin overdose. In her analysis of feminist politics and performance Rosi Braidotti writes that the 'face is a landscape of power', especially when it is 'recognizable, consumable ... it engenders individual and collective identities'.[5] On a 1969 poster for a gig with the Grateful Dead at the Fillmore East, New York, Joplin's face – pockmarked, wild hair, eyes closed – epitomizes the raw abandon of her music and her image as a proto-feminist rock icon, laying down the template for many singers who followed in her wake. In the 1970s Patti Smith, for instance, created her own fusion of beat poetry and rock'n'roll and, like Joplin, had a visual image that was defiantly individual. The bold, androgynous Robert Mapplethorpe photograph of Smith on the cover of her 1975 debut album, *Horses*, perfectly captures that spirit. Rock photographer Pennie Smith said that Smith was one of the women she most enjoyed photographing 'because she never worried about looking pretty'. Then in the 1990s UK artist PJ Harvey reimagined the blues through the prism of post punk, echoing Joplin's abandon in her performance.[6]

As Braidotti argues, 'face is visual commodity' and rebel divas either reject that commodification (as did Joplin) or turn it into an ironic statement, as Debbie Harry did in the 1970s with the cartoon pop art of Blondie. Rooted in the

Poster by David Edward Byrd advertising Janis Joplin's concert at the Fillmore East, New York, 1969

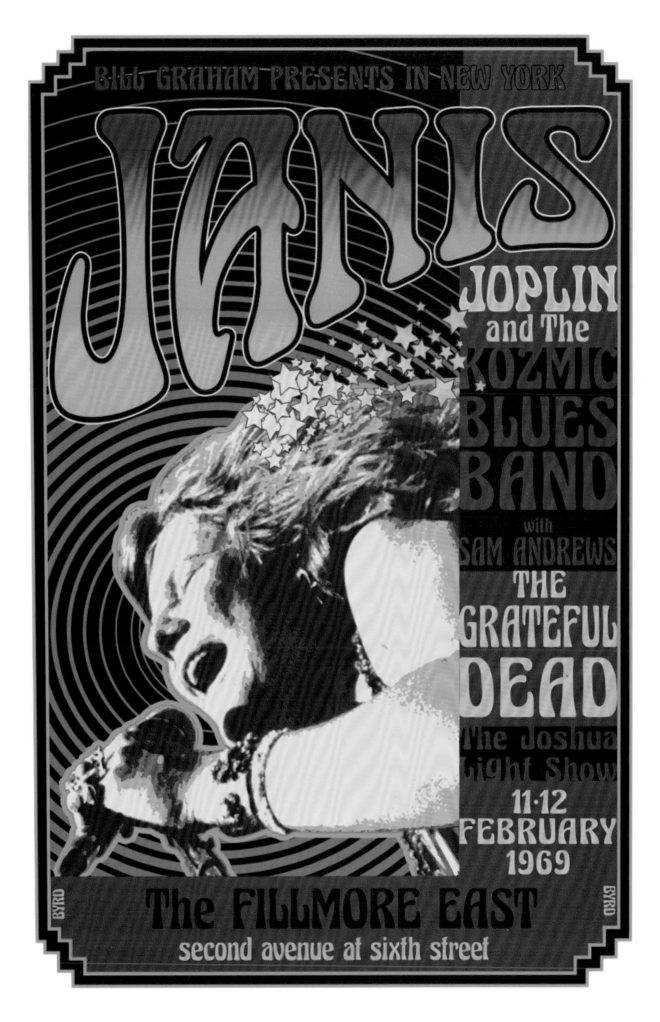

126

*Patti Smith*, 1979. Photograph by Robert Mapplethorpe
V&A: PH.1199-1980

Left:
Brian Maloney, image depicting Deborah Harry from Blondie for *Zig Zag* magazine, no. 98, February 1980
V&A: S.3643-1995

glam punk and new wave scene of New York's Lower East Side, Harry told me in 2007 that the band were 'trying to be uncool'. Despite selling seven million copies of their 1978 breakthrough album *Parallel Lines*, Harry never had a stylist and consciously danced in an awkward, jerky style.

> I didn't want to be showbiz, I didn't like the idea of choreographed routines. I found that nauseating. I still find those cheerleader-like dances completely abnormal ... It didn't concern me that I should be on the right foot with the right beat.[7]

She also resisted attempts by their manager to sack the band and promote Harry as a sexy solo artist, hence the 'BLONDIE IS A GROUP' badge that was worn by fans with pride. Harry took control of the promotional process by projecting her own image – a combination of ice-cold punk and 1940s film star glamour.

Punk was a liberating space for the pop diva, especially performers like Siouxsie Sioux, who projected a dark, dramatic elegance through different incarnations – from the black, spikey hair and chiming chords of 'Hong Kong Garden' in 1978 to the sleek 2000s catwoman image, with a sheer bodysuit made by punk DIY designer Pam Hogg. From the moment in 1976 when she stepped on stage at London's 100 Club with Sid Vicious and improvised an atonal version of the Lord's Prayer, Sioux was as inventive with her music as she was her visual style. As frontwoman of the Banshees she had a freewheeling dance and sang with a soaring yet gutteral call. Throughout the 1980s the Banshees racked up Top 20 hits that combined acid psychedelia, punk pop and goth. 'Whenever the Banshees had a hit I'd think, ooh, we sneaked in that one', she said. 'In the beginning I felt like we'd gate-crashed someone else's party. I'm proud of being part of something that was so innocent, a spontaneous combustion'.[8]

At the heart of rebel reinvention are disruptive divas willing to defy rules of gender and music genre. When Sioux sang 'Happy House' on *Top of the Pops* with menacing sarcasm in 1980, she disrupted a commercial environment that demanded female vocalists be saccharine and sweet. Lori Burns and Mélisse Lafrance define the disruptive diva as adopting 'marginal, countercultural positions in and through their creative work'.[9] Disruptive divas may unsettle

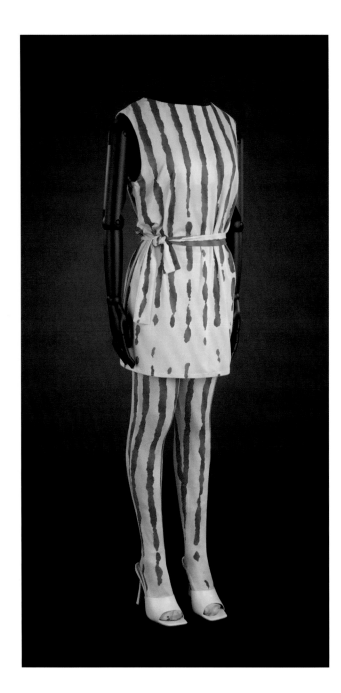

Dress designed by Stephen Sprouse, worn
by Debbie Harry on Blondie's European Tour,
1979
V&A: S.283-1980

the listener and also refuse to stay in one place, driven by a restless creativity and sense of reinvention.

Although Madonna records music that is melodic, harmonic, rhythmic and pleasing, she frequently disrupts the communication of it with provocative statements or hypersexual images undercut with a feminist narrative. For Madonna, visual signs become totems – the crucifix, the Boy Toy belt and, perhaps most iconic of all, the pink cone bra and corset she wore for 1990s Blond Ambition World Tour (p. 131). Designed by Jean Paul Gaultier, it re-purposed the corset from a symbol of feminine submission to something that was spikey, assertive and weaponized. The corset was a spectacular event, an example of Madonna's reinvention from the touselled hair and New York street style of her 'Like A Virgin' era to the sculpted muscles and fierce, streamlined control of Blond Ambition. Musically, too, she was becoming more adventurous, moving from the retro pop of *True Blue* (with its Warholian album cover) to the more personal, questing lyrics of *Like a Prayer*, where she re-evaluated her Catholic upbringing. This laid the groundwork for the deep, autobiographical flow of her highly acclaimed triptych of albums *Ray of Light* (1998), *Music* (2000) and *American Life* (2003).

Madonna's work focuses on female fantasy, ambition and desire, and in her 60s she continues to provoke, refusing to age gracefully and disappear from the pop scene. In May 2022, for example, she collaborated on a NFT (non-fungible token) project with graphic artist Mike Winkelmann, posing naked while giving birth to butterflies, trees and robot insects. All proceeds from the project, which was called *Mother of Creation*, went to National Bail Out, Voices of Children and global activist movement V-Day. 'I'm doing what women have been doing since the beginning of time, which is giving birth', she said. 'On a more existential level I'm giving birth to art and creativity and we would be lost without both.'[10]

The rebel diva often has a defiant, almost shamanic energy that's rooted in a refusal to be constrained. Lady Gaga's work, for instance, has an intersectionality and gender fluidity that allows fans to read her in myriad ways. She has done this through reinvention, creating a character that has freed her from time, place and family heritage, with room to explore colliding ideas. Born and raised in New York City, Stefani Germanotta developed her alter ego

Debbie Harry reading *The Sun,* 28 December
1979. Photograph by Chris Stein

Following pages:
*Siouxsie in Tartan*, 1978/9. Photograph by
Sheila Rock

Madonna wearing a Jean Paul Gaultier cone
bra and corset on the Blond Ambition World
Tour, Feyenoord Stadium, Rotterdam,
July 1990

Madonna attends the Dolce & Gabbana and
The Cinema Society screening of the Epix
World premiere of 'Madonna: The MDNA
Tour' at The Paris Theater, New York, 2013

Madonna performs live after the 64th
annual Eurovision Song Contest, Tel Aviv
Fairgrounds, 2019

Lady Gaga in the early 2000s while performing classic rock covers on the Lower East Side. Taking her name from the Queen song 'Radio Ga Ga', she combined neo-burlesque go-go dancing with metallic drums and electronic club pop to create 2007s *The Fame*. This debut album was a statement on Gaga's method: to mix music, songwriting and performance art with 'fashion, and technology, and pop culture into one performance and then make it commercial'.[11]

Ashanka Kumari defines renaming as performative: 'Through the act of renaming, we can move away from or appropriate new ideas about ourselves. Renaming can be disruptive and a means to regain agency and a new social identity'.[12] Renaming enabled Germanotta to move between girlish melodies and a gruff, robotic voice. As Gaga she had a misfit quality that endeared her to her fans, who were known from the era of her 2009 album *The Fame Monster* as 'Little Monsters'. Her message has always been one of inclusion: freaks, deviants and the marginalized are welcome in Gaga's world. And this is celebrated in the extravagant work of her creative team, Haus of Gaga. Together with fashion director and co-collaborator Nicola Formichetti, Gaga became a muse for innovative designers and built media moments – whether it was the *Telephone* video headpiece designed by Fred Butler, where she becomes a lurid B-movie cartoon, or the custom atelier Versace bodysuit and gold feathered wings by Living Art of Armando on her 2014 Artpop tour.

Eventually Gaga branched out into acting, with film roles in *A Star is Born* (2018) and *House of Gucci* (2021). These Hollywood roles meant another kind of reinvention, moving beyond visual extremity to explore more traditional iterations of divadom.

Rebel reinvention does not always require shock and provocation. Disruptive divas can initiate a huge cultural shift in one subtle statement. Lauryn Hill's 1998 debut solo album, for instance, *The Miseducation of Lauryn Hill*, in its lyrical poetry and graceful interweaving of hip hop, R&B and reggae, ushered in a profound new era of hip hop feminism. 'Seeing Lauryn was seeing ourselves as beautiful, brilliant and bad. Even if we didn't have all that she radiated, we could get there. With Lauryn Hill, it was always more than the music. It was her', said *Essence* Entertainment Director Cori Murray.[13] After success with rap group the

Album cover for *The Miseducation of Lauryn Hill*, artwork based on a photograph by Eric Johnson; art direction by Erwin Gorostiza. Ruffhouse and Columbia Records, 1998

Lady Gaga wearing a headpiece by Fred
Butler in her video for 'Telephone' directed
by Jonas Åkerlund for Interscope Records,
2009

Lady Gaga emerges from an egg-like pod
designed by Haus of Gaga in collaboration
with Hussein Chalayan and made by the Jim
Henson Company, Grammy Awards, 2011

Lady Gaga in an ensemble by Alexander
McQueen arrives at the 2010 MTV Video
Music Awards held at Nokia Theatre, Los
Angeles

Fugees (her crystal clear version of Roberta Flack's 'Killing Me Softly With His Song' dominated mid-1990s radio), 22-year-old Hill wrote, arranged and produced a very personal album exploring anti-racism, motherhood and relationships. After its release the album went to number one on Billboard and was the first rap project to win the Grammy Award for Album of the Year, while the song 'Doo Wop (That Thing)' became the first number one single by a female hip hop artist. With her dreadlocks, Levi jeans and lyrical wordplay, Hill projected an organic, soulful and complex representation of Black womanhood. She was rebelling against the sexual stereotyping of Black women, and the violent imagery of 1990s female rappers like Lil Kim, Foxy Brown and HWA (Hoes With Attitude), whose lyrics were focused on guns, money and sex.

Hill was a quiet diva rebel who withdrew from the limelight after the success of her debut. 'I had to step away when I realized that for the sake of the machine, I was being way too compromised', she said.[14] *The Miseducation of Lauryn Hill* led to her being hailed as the Mother of Hip Hop Reinvention, transforming a male-dominated genre of music that had become locked into tropes of violence, materialism and objectification of women. Calling the album 'an intervention', Black feminist scholar Nicole Horsley sees Lauryn Hill as embodying hip hop feminism, which she defines as 'a radical self-politic of love, empowerment ... and social consciousness for the historically ... erased, and marginalized'.[15]

Missy Elliott, too, is a disruptive diva who opened up new avenues of expression for women of colour. In 1997 her debut album *Supa Dupa Fly* revolutionized hip hop with its staccato beats and surreal rhymes. A plus-size woman, she sent up music industry stereotyping by dancing in an inflated jumpsuit on the video for her breakthrough hit 'The Rain (Supa Dupa Fly)', proving that female artists didn't have to be sylph-like to achieve success (pp. 140–1). Elliott then became a gifted producer as well as rapper, launching her own Goldmind Inc. label and working with artists as varied as Eminem, Destiny's Child, Busta Rhymes and Mariah Carey.

In the UK, rap artist and singer Neneh Cherry showed that there was strength in mixing genres and resisting stereotypes, emerging through the punk club scene of the early 1980s to create 'Buffalo Stance', one of the biggest rap-pop singles of the decade. She is remembered for appearing on *Top of the Pops* aged 25, wearing lycra and trainers and pregnant with her second child. During interviews Cherry recounted the advice her mother gave: 'Don't separate ... the life that you're going to make with this child, from [who] you are and what you want to do'.[16] Saying that 'Buffalo Stance' was about 'surviving and standing strong',[17] Cherry conveyed a picture of young motherhood that was empowering, underlining this with her hands wrapped like a boxer on the cover of her 1989 solo debut *Raw Like Sushi*.

Female artists are often advised to play down the fact that they have children – being a mother makes the female star less marketable. But some rebel divas, like Neneh Cherry and Björk, bring it to the centre of their work. Icelandic artist Björk disrupted the 2001 Academy Awards (where she had been nominated for best song in the Lars von Trier film *Dancer in the Dark*) by wearing a swan dress and dropping an egg on the red carpet. Lady Gaga, too, reflected on birth power for the 2011 Grammy Awards. She was transported along the red carpet inside a giant egg, and then 'hatched out' for a performance of her hit song 'Born This Way' (p. 136). For Björk, themes of nature and motherhood reverberate through her music, particularly on her 2004 album *Medúlla*:

> *Giving birth makes you extremely conscious and you realize that this is the only thing that matters. This primal force ... I wanted to do a vocal album and I wanted it to have a strong feeling of heart, blood and meat.*[18]

Neneh Cherry image used for the cover of her album *Raw Like Sushi*, styled by Judy Blame, 1989. Photograph by Jean-Baptiste Mondino

Following pages:
Stills from Missy Elliott's music video 'The Rain (Supa Dupa Fly)', in which she wears a patent leather inflatable suit, styled by June Ambrose, 1997

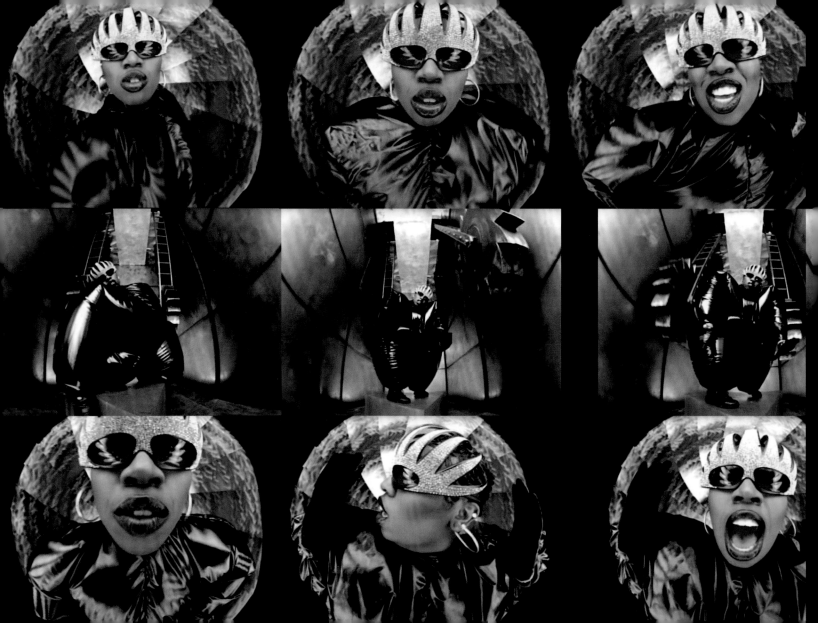

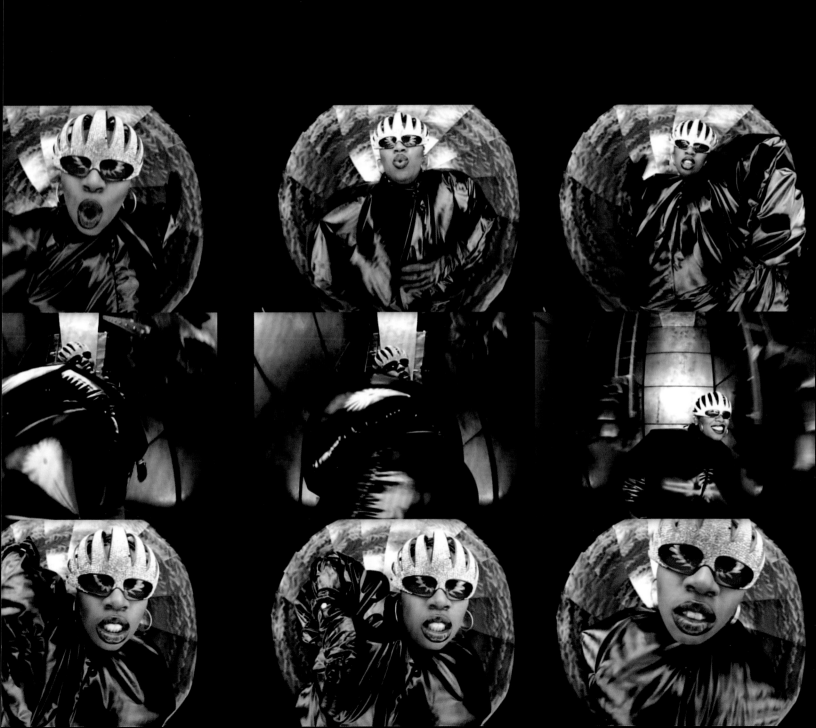

In later projects such as *Biophilia* (2011) and *Utopia* (2017), Björk has explored themes of biology, technology and the ecosphere, creating fantastical visual as well as musical worlds. Embroidery artist James Merry has been one of her key collaborators, creating, for instance, the lace and pearl mask she wore through her 2015 Vulnicura tour and the mask worn with her Sphaera dress for the Cornucopia tour. 'I'm fixated on the idea of something from one world transforming into something from another world – that moment when it's not quite clear which world it's in', Merry enthused.[19]

Futurist divas working in electronic music find limitless room for reinvention – whether it's Björk's Icelandic folktronica, or Canadian artist Grimes (aka Claire Boucher) with her dream pop avatars and cyberpunk soundscapes. 'I don't wanna be just like the face of this thing I built, I want to be the one who built it', she said in 2015.[20] Fascinated by the intersection between music and games, in 2021 she built her own Grimes Metaverse Super Beta on the social platform Discord. As a producer, video maker and musician, Grimes is the architect of her world, reinventing herself in several spheres.

Singer-songwriter Tahlia Debrett Barnett, known as FKA Twigs, also draws on sci-fi themes and abstract electronica to create unsettling visual images. In the video for her 2013 debut single 'Water Me', animated crystal teardrops flowed from her eyes, while for her 2019 Magdalene show she designed with Ed Marler a dreamlike headdress that contrasted with punk knickers, echoing her sonic mix of trip-hop, medieval chant and industrial emo (overleaf). Using an outsider figure like Mary Magdalene was a rebellious act in itself. To FKA Twigs, Magdalene represents the Madonna/whore complex, someone who was judged worthless and stripped of her agency as a woman. Yet, she argues, embodying both sides is when women are at their most powerful. 'When I have been at my most ungraceful, confused, fractured. I stopped judging myself and at that moment found hope in "magdalene". To her I am forever grateful.'[21] Disruptive divas of the 2020s are at home with technology and their work frequently mashes music genre and defies category.

Billie Eilish is one of the latest rebel divas to test the boundaries of image and music. When she first emerged in 2016 with the song 'Ocean Eyes', Eilish seemed like just another dreamy teenage LA singer-songwriter. But together with her brother Finneas O'Connell she drew on trap and industrial pop to create the darkly humorous album *When We All Fall Asleep, Where Do We Go?*, her vocoder voice looped through effects and filters. Combining text and Instagram word-speak in her lyrics to craft a girl-positive emotional world, Eilish has slowly become an alternative global icon. Her shows are filled with raucous mosh-pits of girls chanting her sardonic anthems and wearing baggy street-style fashion (p. 145). Eilish has proved that the modern diva can sell records without hypersexualized videos and still attract an army of fans.

Rebel divas are a dynamic force at the centre of the music industry – their inventiveness, self-expression and refusal to be side-tracked is what drives the future of pop music. In their collaborations with art and fashion and fantasy they make music that is ever richer, more colourful and more empowered.

Björk performing in the Sphaera dress by Iris Van Herpen, with mask by James Merry, for her Cornucopia tour, The Shed, New York, 2019. Photograph by Santiago Felipe

FKA Twigs at her Magdalene live show,
Fabrique, Milan, 2019

Billie Eilish wearing a Stella McCartney 'blue
meanies' outfit at Glastonbury Festival, 2019

# I Want to Break Free: Liberating the Diva

Sasha Geffen

In 2010 Karin Dreijer took the stage at the Norwegian awards ceremony P3 Gold to accept an award for their debut self-titled album as Fever Ray. A sheer red veil covered their face; when they removed it to thank the crowd, they revealed a full-face prosthetic designed to look like molten flesh. Their mouth was hidden; for a moment, they stared into the camera, moaned as if in pain, and then handed the microphone back to the show's host.[1]

Awards shows such as these typically provide musicians with the opportunity to shore up attention on their work – to prove to audiences that they, as people, deserve whatever accolades might rain down on them. They are windows for artists to solidify their public personas and add new chapters to the ongoing narratives that halo them as celebrities, whether major or minor. Dreijer stepped up to this plate playing a modified game. Rather than accept a televised appearance as a chance for viewers and listeners to know them better, to hear more about the effort that went into making the winning album or the people who had been important to them in their life, they thickened the shell around them. They declined to show their face or speak a single word. The moment endures thanks to their refusal of the usual terms of engagement.

Across the history of recorded music, the diva perches on a spectacular paradox. Like all celebrities, she is both one and she is multiple. She is a ubiquitous image stemming from a rarified source – someone who lives, embodied, like mortals, and yet must negotiate with the world's insatiable hunger for evidence of her living. What sets the diva apart is her ability to take her own image and hold it aloft – to toy with the image as material. The diva's the one who charges the feedback loop to the point of screaming. Her power derives from the vanishing point between the revealed and the obscured: the Lycra that concludes the plunging neckline, the crease of skin at the edge of the mask.

In a mass media market, the reproduction and distribution of the diva's form only concentrates its value. Ubiquity increases fervour before it gives way to

exhaustion. As Shannon Marcus writes in her 2019 study *The Drama of Celebrity*,

> *The economy of celebrity does not operate according to a simple metric of supply and demand in which the more images there are of a star, the less value they have. Instead, once the star has secured the public and press's interest ... the more copies, the more celebrity. With each new series of multiples, the celebrity becomes all the more singular ... By virtue of being multiplied, celebrities come to seem unique; their apparent singularity is intensified by copying. Copies do not dim the celebrity's halo; they brighten it.[2]*

Marcus traces the origins of celebrity culture to advances in physical transportation and image reproduction in the nineteenth century, when theatre stars such as Sarah Bernhardt negotiated with an attentive, enthusiastic public to cultivate lifelong renown. In the twentieth century the recording industry added a new dimension to the phenomenon of the star. Records captured, severed and multiplied voices from their point of origin, drawing the diva's voice in to the home of the listener alongside her image. As technologies for reproducing and proliferating sound and image accelerated through the twentieth and twenty-first centuries, the diva has adapted. She has grown more canny and more challenging in assuming her larger-than-life station in popular culture. A product of the feedback loop between origin and amplification, she is not strictly human, and as such, she's not strictly bound by human categories. That makes it easier for her to slip outside the constricts of systems like gender, to point at their limits once she's outside them and to invite her audiences to dream up new rules.

Throughout the 1960s, the *Ike and Tina Turner Revue* sent their electrified R&B performances beaming into living rooms across the United States. Having developed their incendiary act on tour, the group took full advantage of the medium of television as they played slots on the expanding circuit of mid-century music shows. In their performances, Tina and her Ikettes sang and moved in ways that veered from conventions around Black women's televised presences at the time. Unlike Motown groups like the Supremes or girl groups like the Shirelles, whose subtle, slight movements on

Contact sheet of studio portraits of Tina Turner, New York, 1969

stage hewed to a preconceived model of respectability, Tina danced with abandon. Her performances easily captured the camera's adoration. She and her backing singers wore fringed, sparkling dresses and long, loose wigs that trailed and multiplied their dextrous movements.

From the beginning of her career, Tina Turner nurtured a canny understanding of mass media's potential for manipulation. The costuming and choreography of the *Revue* both dazzled the eye and amplified the way the grain of her voice hit the ear. In her 2020 book *Black Diamond Queens*, Maureen Mahon writes:

> On stage, she paired her passionate vocals with a physicality that functioned as a delivery system for the sexuality that had long animated rock and roll. Tina and her backing vocalists, the Ikettes, dressed in revealing stage costumes and performed an almost continuous flurry of hip-shaking, go-go-style dance steps. Wigs gave them swinging, shoulder-length tresses that accentuated their explosive movements.[3]

The optics and kinetics of Tina's costumes had the effect of nearly doubling each step of her dances. Whenever she moved her hips to the right, strings of sparkling beads would follow. When she switched to the left, the sudden reversal showed in the shock of oscillating fabric. Tina lengthened and exaggerated her own movements with the clothes she wore on stage, which served as a physical amplification system similar to the electric networks that heightened her vocal roar.

This direct engagement with the TV camera would inform generations of pop and rock stars to come, many of whom – like Mick Jagger – would fashion their vocal

Sequinned dress worn by Tina Turner
designed by Shirley Ann Russell, 1975
V&A: S.95-1992

approach and physicality directly after Tina Turner. As her influence trailed long through the 1970s, her own star began to diminish. In 1976 she left her viciously abusive husband. Turner began the process of establishing herself as a solo performer towards the end of the 1970s but found herself thwarted by a recording industry that assumed she had already run her course. To stay afloat financially, she booked solo shows in Las Vegas and commissioned designer Bob Mackie to create a new look for her new chapter.

Mackie riffed on the dresses that Turner had tweaked for herself and the Ikettes during her time in the *Revue*. Sparkling fringe was a must, though he crafted it from metal rather than beads to make sure that it would survive the firestorm of her dancing. To the silver trails dangling from the dress he added two enormous lamé wings. 'I looked like I was about to take flight and soar – which was exactly how I felt about being on my own for the first time', Turner wrote in her 2020 autobiography, *That's My Life*.[4] The freedom of movement she had exercised on stage with the Revue expanded to fill her life. By the mid-1980s Turner returned to the spotlight as a star in her own right with the multi-platinum album *Private Dancer*.[5]

Turner's strategic manipulation of live performance and televised media would inform other divas' approach to the visual dimensions of their music, especially as the music video crystallized as an art form in its own right. In the autumn of 1975 the British rock band Queen released their breakthrough single 'Bohemian Rhapsody', a six-minute chimera of a song that leapt from pop ballad to operatic crescendo to progressive rock finale. Although Queen had enjoyed some measure of success in both the United Kingdom and the United States in the first half of the 1970s, 'Bohemian Rhapsody' marked their first entry into stardom proper. Bolstering its bold turns was a meticulous studio ethic. The voices heard in the song are not simply the voices of the band members inscribed on tape; they're three-part harmonies doubled, tripled, quintupled to the era's technological limits. Freddie Mercury's (1946–1991) distinctive lead vocals track back on themselves, chased by Brian May and Roger Taylor, until a whole choir appears from thin air.

When it came time to promote 'Bohemian Rhapsody', Queen opted out of lip-syncing along to its auditory smoke and mirrors on *Top of the Pops*. Instead, they

Freddie Mercury rousing the crowd in
Wembley Stadium, London, at Queen's
1986 concert. Photograph by Denis O'Regan

Freddie Mercury at *Live Aid*, 1985.
Photograph by Kent Gavin

filmed a dreamlike visual in which their images multiplied kaleidoscopically alongside their voices. While record companies were no strangers to using promotional videos in support of singles, most tended to collage together footage of bands performing, either live or in the studio or both. Most videos courted verisimilitude, giving viewers the chance to connect the sound of a song with the process behind making it. The video for 'Bohemian Rhapsody' does feature some live shots of Mercury performing in an angelic white satin shrug, but its most indelible sequences better simulate the experience of hearing the song rather than playing it. Queen amplified the fantasy of the multi-tracked voice by multiplying their faces. At one point, during a cascading overdub that's impossible to sing with only one throat, Mercury's singing visage gets trailed by a line of shrinking, electric blue copies. Rather than obscure the fantasy of multiple Mercuries singing all at once, tethering the multiple voice back to a singular source, Queen insist on their lead singer's multiplicity.

'Bohemian Rhapsody' and its video proved internationally sensational. 'The song reached No 1 and stayed there for nine weeks, ensuring videos would henceforth be a mandatory tool in the marketing of music', writes Keith Cameron in the *Guardian*.[6] The video's fluid fantasy presaged the MTV era by half a decade, and would serve as a touchstone as legions of British new wave and synthpop bands vied for airtime on the American cable network. Videos like 'I Ran (So Far Away)' by A Flock of Seagulls, with its hall of mirrors reflecting the band, unfolded in response to Queen's solution to the problem of their own vocal proliferation.

If the diva, as a pop cultural phenomenon, electrifies the space between the performer and her audience, few rock frontmen were better suited to the role than Mercury. As a recording artist and producer, he deftly wielded his own voice not as a singular force but as an environmental enclosure, reproduced by multitracking and abundant use of delay effects, as on the extended a cappella breakdown on 'The Prophet's Song', where distinctive vocal takes loop back on themselves, contradicting their own uniqueness. The logics of mass production circulated through Queen's music. In a 2005 retrospective on the band for *Uncut*, Jon Wilde writes, 'If the band were accused of shallowness, [Mercury would] say: "Of course, dear. We're wonderfully

shallow. Our songs are like Bic razors. Designed for mass consumption and instantly disposable".'[7]

These gestures deviated from the masculine ideal of singular genius, or the idea that rock stars wield power by imposing their uniqueness on submissive masses. Mercury's visual and vocal androgyny – the ways he celebrated his own queerness in plain sight – tapped an understanding of his own celebrity as reciprocal with the adoration of his audience. The current of Queen's music, whether in the studio or on stage, flowed freely from source to recipient. During the band's iconic Live Aid performance in 1985, Mercury led the crowd in a singalong of increasingly complex melodic phrases. He conducted the longest note with a fist held aloft, moving in sync with a crowd of tens of thousands. The sequence is so beloved it has its own track marker on YouTube, titled 'Aye-Oh'.[8] With each utterance of the crowd, Mercury throws his head back as if drinking up the sound – absorbing his own echo and echoing it back in an energetic loop that threatens to dissolve celebrity's pedestal, challenging the differences between people as a whole.

Like Turner and Mercury, 1980s video stars such as Grace Jones understood their own voices and images as entities separate from their bodies themselves, material that could be exaggerated and distorted past the point of realism. Born in Spanish Town, Jamaica, Jones began her career as a model in New York before releasing her debut album in 1977. Together with her artistic and romantic partner Jean-Paul Goude, she cultivated an image of otherworldly androgyny through striking photographs and videos. The cover to her 1985 album *Slave to the Rhythm* depicts an elongated scream, with Jones's mouth horizontally extended and pixelated via copied and pasted slices of the same photograph. In her music videos, she similarly copied her own face to uncanny effect. The video for the single 'Private Life' shows her removing a lifelike mask of her own face, revealing a stoic, mask-like expression beneath. In 'Demolition Man', a video taken from the cheekily titled 1982 collection *A One Man Show*, she commands a small army of clones all wearing the same mask.

Jones confronted the strangeness of photographic image reproduction by duplicating herself within the frame. She also toyed with taboos around the human body and its strange charge as the focal point of celebrity. In

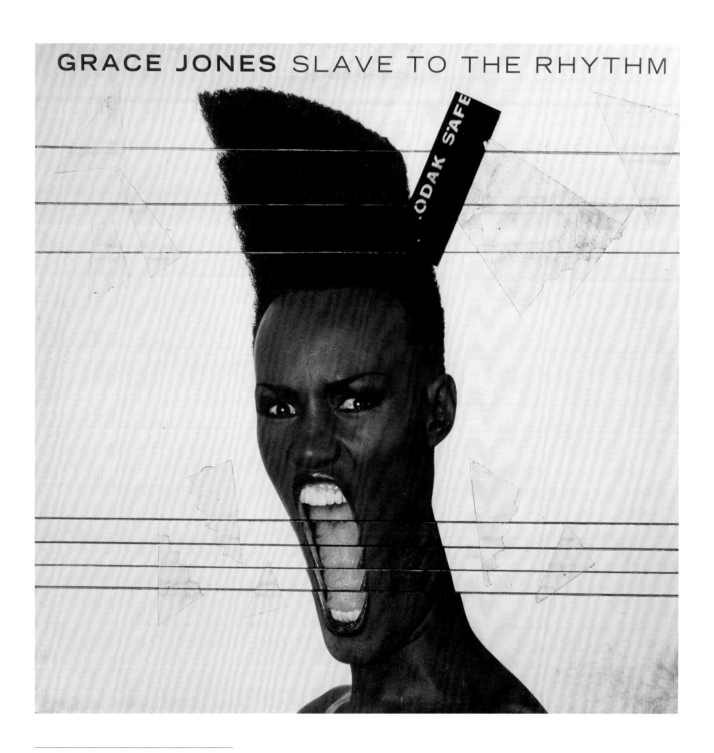

Album cover for Grace Jones, *Slave to the Rhythm*, designed by Jean-Paul Goude.
Island Records, 1985

live performances in the early 1980s, Jones would wear a breastplate decorated with convincing replicas of actual breasts (p. 146). Gendered conventions dictated that she could not perform topless like men, that breasts could only be visually perceived in certain circumstances with certain dangerous implications. In response to this boundary, Jones masked her torso the same way she masked her face: a lifelike copy covering up the real thing. The costume skirted the taboo while highlighting its absurdity. The public demands images of celebrities, but only certain parts that stay dry of pornography's muddied waters. In her probing gaze, Jones seems to ask: 'it's all image; what's the difference?'

The dance between masking and revealing would prove a productive one for the diva in the continuing era of video. In 1992, the tenured diva Prince issued the single 'My Name is Prince', a hip hop declaration of identity accompanied by a costume that obscured the star's face. On the single art and in the music video Prince wore a police hat with chain mail dangling from the brim, a visual echo of Tina Turner's swaying, metallic dresses and an ancestor to the fringed masks now worn by queer country performer Orville Peck. Glimpses of Prince's face slipped between the chains as he moved but the hat largely concealed his most distinctive features. In 1993 Prince wore a similar hat while performing 'My Name is Prince' on the Act I tour, and sold replicas of the costume piece as merchandise. Fans could shell out for a shard of his diva's halo not by resembling him, exactly, but by resembling no one in the same way he did – by donning the same disguise. It's a gesture that complements the sight gag of Jones's breastplate: Jones toyed with her celebrity by displaying plastic copies of forbidden body parts, while Prince did the same by covering up the part of his body most focal to his stardom.

In the twenty-first century, in an age of on-demand streaming video, divas have continued to avail themselves of this playful pulse between coveted and forbidden zones of the gendered body. Through their mutable performances in highly produced music videos, pop stars

Prince performing in his 'chain hat' at Radio City Music Hall, March 1993

like Nicki Minaj and Lady Gaga have wholly embraced the artificiality of the diva's place in culture, refusing the terms of authenticity by doubling down on the fake. Minaj's bubblegum-pink wigs and adoption of the nickname 'Barbie' serve as knowing nods to the mass production of her own image, while Gaga's more grotesque takes on the diva's stance have included prosthetic horns bulging from foreheads (overleaf), digitally enlarged eyes and a pair of LED sunglasses flashing out the words 'POP CULTURE'. The diva wears her own screens, conscious of the trillions of pixels that will recreate her.

Alongside Gaga, other queer artists have both assumed and challenged the role of the diva and the images that multiply infinitely around her body. In the 2018 video for the song 'PYNK', the nonbinary performer Janelle Monáe dons a pair of bright pink 'pussy' pants alongside her dancers: a garment that reproduces and exaggerates another part of the diva's body that's forbidden to display directly (p. 159). Furthering the logic of Grace Jones's breastplate, Monáe toys with one of mass culture's most taboo images, turning it into a camp sight gag that's emphasized by the video's winking choreography. Monáe released the video during the same album cycle that she came out as pansexual; its visual exaggerations circumvent apprehensions about depicting queer intimacy by overshooting and showing outrageous queer play. Tessa Thompson, the actress rumoured to be Monáe's girlfriend at the time, pops her head between the singer's legs and smiles. The folds of the simulated vagina elongate the dancers' movements in a similar way to the fringe on the Ikettes' dresses, amplifying a body part that – like the diva herself – is simultaneously hidden and overexposed.

What if the diva's whole body could shiver like a garment in the wake of her movement? That question hovers around the work of artists SOPHIE (1986–2021) and Arca, both of whom have created simulations of not just body parts but their entire bodies in recent videos. In SOPHIE's video for 'FACESHOPPING', the UK-born electronic artist renders herself in computer animation, then toys with the render as though it were a rubber balloon. It inflates, deflates, bounces, twists; it's sliced into vertical segments (p. 160) that then topple on the floor of an undelineated blank space. Between these shots, the video inserts rapid-fire clips of makeup shelves, social media logos,

raw meat, and skin cells: the flesh brushing up against the tools of its inflection. For SOPHIE, who became known as a transfeminine artist in the months before the video was released, the body is not organic material moulded into an artificial shape. The border between the natural and the fabricated collapses here. The body is a plastic confluence of social meaning, a communicative plane constantly modulated by collective perception.

In videos accompanying her recent Kick album cycle, the Venezuelan producer and Björk protégé Arca similarly

recreates herself in imaginative virtual space. 'Nonbinary' casts her as a technologically enhanced Venus rising from polluted waters inside a clamshell. In 'Prada/Rakata' she plays a roster of posthuman monsters, from double-headed angels with molluscs for genitals to a six-limbed biomechanical mother dangling an amber eggsac between her legs. One sequence shows her half-formed and enormous inside a construction scaffold, a colossus being built (p. 161). One leg turns into a mermaid's tail; one arm culminates in a rocket launcher covered in graffiti, the word 'DIVA' clearly legible on its stock.

Here, the diva's constructed nature rises to the fore. Arca builds herself in this computer-generated dreamscape: enormous, monstrous, fabulous. The historic exchange between source and image falters; it's no longer clear that there is anyone generating the replicated image. The image itself appears self-sustaining; it is its own source. And if there is no originating body, no real person against which to check the copy, then the diva can be anything. She can iterate herself beyond patterns like hegemonic gender. As the mask behind the mask behind the mask, she can blink herself free.

Still from Janelle Monáe's video for 'PYNK', (directed by Emma Westenberg), ensemble designed by Duran Lantink, 2018

Left:
Artwork for Lady Gaga, *Born this Way*, designed by Gaga with stylist Nicola Formichetti, 2011. Photograph by Nick Knight

Still from SOPHIE's music video
'FACESHOPPING' directed in collaboration
with Aaron Chan, 2018

Still from Arca's music video 'Prada/Rakata',
2021. Concept and scenario by Frederik
Heyman and Arca; 3D visual creation by
Frederik Heyman; symbolic gestation by
Alejandra Ghersi
Produced by: Bounce Rocks & Shaun
MacDonald; Management: XLrecordings

# By Myself:
## Negotiating the Public and the Private

Miranda Sawyer

From the start, there is the voice. A diva's instrument, and, vitally, it comes from her very self. Her talent, made from and of her, brimming with her life, her loves, failures, desires, disasters. When she sings, we don't need to know exactly what happened, because the voice reveals all. 'I want to make people cry', said Edith Piaf, 'even if they don't understand my words',[1] and this is the diva's power. We cry because she sings of our lives. We second that emotion.

We know this, even when we're young. Watch a toddler swoon or storm to 'drivers license' or 'About Damn Time', throw themselves into becoming a living version of what they hear. Music, especially pop music, precious emotion in a cheap wrapper, shoots an arrow directly into our hearts. And into our lives: a pop song winds around our memories, it patterns our desires, tracks our most significant times, whether full of joy or smashed with heartbreak. Unlike film or books or theatre, with their timed, rigid storylines, there's room within music for our own lives to exist. Our experiences can shimmer between the notes and the lyrics. 'Anyone Who Had A Heart' means something to you and something different to me and something different to Dusty Springfield (1939–1999) herself. And it's in that duality – that ability to create something absolutely meaningful for both singer and listener – that lies at the heart of our relationship with the diva. We're separate, but we overlap. As Sade once said: 'The music ... is actually owned by the person who takes it into their life. It's their music then. It's not me singing to them. It's their own soundscape, their own soundtrack to their lives.'[2] It isn't an illusion: the singer truly is singing both her song and ours.

And so, the boundaries between us can become blurred. Is she us, are we her? If a diva creates something so beautiful about our lives, if she knows our deepest emotions and sings our feelings to the world, if she understands us so well, do we also understand her and her life? Should we? Should we know everything about a diva's private life, because her work reveals us so intimately? After all, when Dusty was singing so poignantly about her lost loves, she was hiding her true sexuality. The diva's voice invites us in, but how close can we get?

We might feel we understand her, but we also know that she's more than us. More beautiful, more sensitive. And definitely more dramatic. Divas' stories are more epic than ours. Piaf also said, 'if I did not live the life that I did,

I would not be able to sing the way I do',[3] and that is true of all divas. Divas exist to live the full gamut of romantic experience. To go through life's turmoils and triumphs, and report back. A true diva not only has a layer of protective armour missing, she has a courage few of us can muster. No point in dwelling on the many who find the world so overwhelming that they turn to drink and drugs to dull the extremes. Instead, let's think of how sensitive someone must be to be forced to do that. (As Liza Minnelli said, 'all drunks go to heaven, because they've been through hell on earth'.[4]) With a true diva, we get an artist who seems so close when she performs that she gives expression to our innermost souls; but who is also far wilder, braver and more magnificent than we could ever be, sweeping through a significant life, drowning in its depths and soaring to its heights in a mythic manner. Glamorous, gritty, facing her troubles with an award-winning smile and a frock to die for. To quote Minnelli again, 'Reality is something you rise above'.[5]

As we know, many divas spin the drama of their lives into their lyrics, some more directly and beautifully than others. Adele dived into the wreck of her marriage and emerged with songs, on 30, which epitomize the broken-hearted lament of any devastated friend. Billie Eilish transformed incessant media commentary about her body into 'Not My Responsibility'; the treatment of her and her young friends by older men into 'Your Power'. Amy Winehouse (1983–2011) flipped her love affairs into wit ('You Should Be Stronger Than Me') or poignancy. In 'Back To Black', every line rings like a bell: 'Life is like a pipe and I'm a tiny penny rolling up the walls inside.' Such lyrics draw us even closer. We feel the heartbreak in the voice, but once we learn the words, we're even more enraptured.

And to help with our identification with her, a diva is always a solo artist. Beyoncé started in Destiny's Child, but it's on her own that she is recognized. Dusty Springfield was in The Springfields before going solo; Sade has a band, but it's under her name; Debbie Harry's nickname (Blondie) named the whole band, though it's only her we think of. We like our divas to be alone. Solo talent, when it comes to women singers, is definitely what the record industry prefers. Perhaps it feeds into the ancient myth of a lone woman needing to be saved from the world (here I am! says the record company, sweeping in on a noble

Liza Minnelli performs at the Wolf Trap,
Virginia, 1980

steed: your protector! And here is the loving support I can provide for you! Just sign here...). But maybe it's the flip-side, too: the assumption that a lone woman will be more easily managed or manipulated than, for instance, a band made up of young men. Though you wonder if anyone thought that through when it came to, say, the fiery, unpredictable Amy Winehouse, who could take down ten glum indie groups with a single kohl-flicked eye roll. Or Dusty Springfield, who said, 'I was an invention, but my own invention. I was my own Svengali'.[6] Still, if the talent is just one person, then we focus on that voice; the band is a backing band, there to highlight the central performance. We score our emotional hit, our musical high, delivered in its purest single form.

It's interesting to note how the singer's ability to take the personal and turn it into the universal in her art extends into the way fans experience music. Each of us can enjoy music alone, at home, in bed, on headphones while in tears on the 159 bus... but also communally, with other devotees, in a vast, united love. At a concert, as a fan you are a single drop in a torrent, an emotional outpouring. You can feel it in the room. It's noisy, both personal and communal, an energy that moves between the artist and the audience. This is not the relationship between a fan and a movie star, or a fine artist – though the love, especially for film stars, can be profound. For those, the adoration has to be distanced, an emotion experienced in a different room to the artist herself. But if an artist performs on stage, with an audience present... And if that performer gives her all, without a script, not acting, not pretending to be someone else, but offering her own seemingly spontaneous self and her true gift... Then we, as the audience, every individual and all of us together, respond accordingly. The love is tangible. Everyone can feel it. Interestingly, this magic happens whether or not the diva sings her own words or someone else's. The authenticity she brings and sings is felt completely by the audience: Dusty Springfield performs Hal David's words with the same emotional truth as Amy Winehouse sings her self-penned lyrics. A diva can interpret lyrics, wear personalities, like outfits, to highlight and accentuate the essential truth.

Despite such closeness between audience and diva, it's impossible to imagine what it's like to be swamped by so much love in one room: all that emotion coming for you – only you! – and your talent. An audience gives a diva a love that very few of us will experience. Not just an ordinary love, a greater one. A love so big – so wide, so deep – that it swamps any offered by one person: a never-ending, unchanging, undying devotion. A diva needs fans, not just for her bank balance but to provide this, the greatest love of all. And yes, that is a reference to Whitney Houston (1963–2012). There are many YouTube videos of Whitney singing that very song live: in the UK, in Italy, in Chile, at a Nelson Mandela tribute. In every context, she sings it to her fans (another example of a diva turning a song into what we each want it to mean: it was originally recorded by George Benson for a 1977 Muhammed Ali biopic).

It's this search for love that leads a diva to her fame. It doesn't matter that others may love her, she needs that Big Love, that connection with fans, to sustain her, drown out the other noise, convince her she is loveable. Even Sade, a controlled and private person who brings albums out without press fanfare, says: 'Whatever anybody says about me, when I feel the warmth from the audiences, I think it's worth all the bullshit.'[7] But love, especially for women, rarely comes without consequences. Women are taught to be grateful for love, to be nice to those who offer it. Even when it's unwanted, too close, too demanding. 'Love me!' scream her fans, and so the diva tries. But how much should a diva give? Everything? How grateful should she be? Does she offer up her private life, her personal time? Where is the line drawn between public and private? Who draws that line? Does it shift? Who shifts it? Can it be maintained?

For years, up until the 1960s, stars were kept utterly apart from their fans, their connection mediated by the press. Interviewers and photographers offered a snapshot of the artist, filtered by opinion and angle, by lighting and spin. And this careful distancing kept the glamour real, the star untouchable. Outside specialized magazine articles or TV appearances, fans were restricted to buying tickets to watch their star's live performances. No wonder we pored over lyrics and posters: there was no chance of getting nearer. You could join a fan club maybe, or dress like your star, perhaps make your way to a premiere, squeeze through the crowds to the front, crush yourself up against the barriers for a glimpse of your special one as she took the few short steps on the red carpet from car to party. If you were really dedicated, you might find out her home

Dusty Springfield in an English television
studio, 1962. Photograph by Harry
Hammond
V&A: S.15302-2009

Following pages:
Whitney Houston performing at Wembley
Arena, London, 1988. Photograph by
David Corio

address, sit on the wall opposite the front door, chat to her mum as she popped out to the shops. Later on in your diva's career, you might walk past the high fence of a gated property and wonder, 'Is she in?'

From the early 1970s, when a fan could wander up to a Beatle's house and be offered a cup of tea,[8] the line of privacy became more rigid. In the early 1990s, Madonna did her jogging with several bodyguards alongside her; Prince hid away in his Paisley Park compound. But, gradually, things morphed. Perhaps there was a sense, in certain parts of the media, that these uppity superstars needed taking down a peg or two. Magazines like *Heat* and *Closer* specialized in taking unwanted paparazzi photographs and using them to turn celebrities back into muggles (in 2004 *Heat* ran a cover devoted to 'Stars' Shock Sweat Patches!'). Reality TV invited famous people to mingle with the not-so-famous and be filmed taking part in humiliating tasks. This also offered a means for the nearly famous to become full household names (*Keeping Up with the Kardashians* is a case in point).

Over the past decade, social media has offered fans seemingly unfiltered – though often actually carefully managed – access to the real person behind the starry façade. Finally, performers have the chance to reach out personally to their armies of devotees, without having to subject themselves to a stupid TV format or hand over power to an editor. Almost every big star is now all over social media, sharing album covers, award wins, photographs of themselves with other stars, all dressed up with somewhere chic to go. Beyoncé is a particular genius at this, but there are many who use social media well. Wonder at FKA Twigs and her back-breaking pole dancing feats! Marvel at Madonna's new outfit while questioning her decision to showcase it from under the bed! You could see how this might seem a better deal for the artist, in terms of promotion. But some also share the more prosaic parts of their lives, let their fans creep closer. Children's party pics, an unpacked suitcase, a work-out regime, a rant about how they feel about political causes or the state of their own marriage. Regularly, we are offered glimpses behind the velvet rope: Lily Allen with her kids at Glastonbury; Jane Fonda getting stuck in her red carpet dress; Drew Barrymore losing her mind over a rain shower.

What democratic delight, reaching new people

without a mediator, talking to your fans directly! Except that, for every devotee who loves you, leaves streams of hearts and thumbs up, there are trolls. Haters, or – is this worse? – those who just don't really care. Comments roll out under every picture, a red carpet of hate and love and disagreement. When Billie Eilish began her career, she was a young teenager, and used Instagram in the manner of a young teenager: to vent, to be funny, to show off, to experiment (overleaf). Her fans joined in. But once she hit the mainstream and became hugely famous, that fan-star intimacy disappeared. It became, she said, 'like if you wanted to whisper a secret to a friend of yours, but while whispering it, they had a microphone in their ear, and it was shooting to 80 million people'.[9]

Eilish also said: 'When it comes to fans, it's complicated. I don't even know where to start. I don't really know how to keep a boundary.'[10] Where to hold back, what to reveal? Where is that boundary line of privacy positioned, the door beyond which no stranger can pass? It keeps moving, shifting outwards and inwards, a wave drawing in and out. Even if, like Sade, you choose to withdraw, fans will spend hours analysing every little detail. And if you're casual about your pictures, then strange obsessions begin to flourish. Britney Spears fans are forensic over every one of her cheerful Instagram pics. Here is Britney lying on the beach with her legs up in the air and her arms straight out. She's making an inverted T! What can this stand for? What does it meeeean?

Image does convey messages, of course. A diva's work image is donned: like armour, is the cliché, or a uniform. Dusty would spend five hours doing her own makeup, donning her wigs (called Cilla, Lulu, Sandie). More usually, there are a couple of hair and make-up artists on hand, a diva's closest companions, on a salary, not a percentage. Hair and make-up know the true person, before the glamour is applied, before the diva wriggles into a gown and steps out on stage. They know the fall-out of an intimate relationship, the difficulties with a body that must age, despite everything. They cover the evidence, hoik and tweak and fit and flip and shade and twist to perfection. They know that image is utterly vital to a diva. Often, her initial public look is designed by management or record company. Usually, it's non-threatening: a good girl, a girl-next-door, a schoolgirl, a little sparrow. No wonder

Madonna and bodyguards jogging outside
Central Park, New York, 1990

Instagram selfie, posted by Billie Eilish,
30 June 2022

A poster signed by #FreeBritney activists
campaigning for Britney Spears' release from
her conservatorship, 2021

The unmistakable silhouette of Sade during
her *Live in Concert*, PNC Arts Center, New
Jersey, 2001

Edith Piaf and Marlene Dietrich, in Piaf's
dressing room in the Versailles Nightclub,
New York, 1952

the diva finds herself confined. She creates another look, helped by her hair and make-up allies. There's a world of difference between a teenager in plaits and a woman with a snake writhing around her; between a hula-hooping b girl and a braided Southern queen. Sade's careful, elegant presentation throughout her career ensured that we knew she meant business. Her silhouette – so recognizable! – conveys her unique sophistication and control (previous page). In contrast, as Amy Winehouse became sicker and her body reduced in size, her beehive became taller and taller, an ever-increasing 'fuck you' to the world.

Because at all points, a diva's body and mind are not completely her own. They belong to others. Talent is a money-making machine and she has to work; even during her off-duty time she has to nourish that talent, maintain her health, eat right, practice. And so, in extremis, a diva may decide to attack her talent or be careless with her body. Recklessness with such gifts is born from a dislike of being controlled; it morphs into disregard for her own health, her own self. And her fans can feel this. They worry about her, they care. Perhaps they can give her the love that will heal...

Which brings us to the terrible moment when such love is taken away. What to do if your fans move on – to another singer, another talent, another diva? The heartbreak is devastating. Whitney Houston was very upset at the very idea of Paula Abdul having a hit.[11] But her fans didn't desert her then. It was in 2010, when she performed in Australia, that they retreated, devastated at what they saw. The same thing happened with Amy Winehouse in Belgrade in 2011. Fans only recoil when a diva loses her way. Perhaps her management has pushed her on stage when she's unwell, or not well prepared, or should be in rehab. The money needs to be made, but she's not up to the challenge. The fans can see the obvious damage, the slide from what she once was. It's too much to witness in someone you love. It's fine if the diva is clearly well in herself – think of Liza Minnelli's recent appearance at Michael Feinstein's special

Surrounded by the press, Amy Winehouse moves out of her London home in 2008, carrying her Sarah Bernhardt mirror with her

concert, where she performed wonderfully, from her chair –
not so much if she is not.

It takes a lot for fans to turn away forever, though. They
may avert their faces if their diva is suffering, or absent,
but they will always be there for her if she is truly there for
them. It was her fans that revived Edith Piaf's career, through
their reaction to her concerts at the Olympia in Paris
between 1955 and 1962. Critics thought she was finished;
the lines of fans said otherwise. When all fails, it's those who
give you love that sustain. Many of our divas are long dead.
The living voice is gone, but it still sings our song, and the
fans will always love you.

Edith Piaf performing at the Paris Olympia,
1961

# Bibliography

Adichie, Chimamanda Nogizi, *We Should All be Feminists* (London 2014)

Blackburn, *Julia, With Billie: A New Look at the Unforgettable Lady Day* (London 2005)

Braidotti, Rosi, 'Punk Women and Riot Grrls', *Performance Philosophy*, vol. 1, no. 1 (2015), pp. 239-54

Braziel, Jana Evans, '"Bye, Bye Baby": Race, Bisexuality, and the Blues in the Music of Bessie Smith and Janis Joplin', *Popular Music and Society*, vol. 27, no. 1 (2004), pp. 3-26

Burns, Lori, and Mélisse Lafrance, *Disruptive Divas Feminism, Identity and Popular Music* (New York and London 2002)

Carey, Mariah, with Michaela Angela Davis, *The Meaning of Mariah Carey* (London 2020)

Cleary, Stephen, *I Put a Spell on You: The Autobiography of Nina Simone* (Cambridge 1991)

Carman, Emily, *Independent Stardom: Freelance Women in the Hollywood Studio System* (Austin 2015)

Cochrane, Kira, *Modern Women: 52 Pioneers* (London 2017)

Cohen, Harvey G., *Duke Ellington's America* (Chicago 2010)

Cowgill, Rachel, and Hilary Poriss, eds, *The Arts of the Prima Donna in the Long Nineteenth Century* (Oxford 2012)

Du Bois, W.E.B., *The Souls of Black Folk* (Chicago 1903)

Friedan, Betty, *The Feminine Mystique* (London 1963)

Geffen, Sasha, *Glitter Up the Dark: How Pop Music Broke the Binary* (Austin 2020)

Gioia, Ted, *The History of Jazz* (Oxford 1997)

Gleason, Ralph J., *Celebrating the Duke: And Louis, Bessie, Billie, Bird, Caren, Miles, Dizzy and Other Heroes* (Boston 1976)

Head, Edith, and Paddy Calistro, *Edith Head's Hollywood* (New York 1983)

Horowitz, Pamela, et al., *Julian Bond's Time to Teach: A History of the Southern Civil Rights Movement* (Boston 2021)

Horsley, M. Nicole, 'Hip Hop Feminism Starter Kit', *Journal of Hip Hop Studies*, vol. 7, no. 1 (summer 2020), pp. 103-15

Huffington, Arianna Stassinopoulos, *Maria Callas: The Woman Behind the Legend* (Lanham, MD, 2002)

John, Elton, *Me* (London 2019)

Jules-Rosette, Bennetta, *Josephine Baker in Art and Life: The Icon and the Image* (Chicago 2007)

Kennedy, Gerrick, *Didn't We Almost Have It All: In Defense of Whitney Houston* (New York 2022)

Kerr, Rosalind, *The Rise of the Diva on the Sixteenth Century Commedia dell' Arte Stage* (Toronto 2015)

Kumari, Ashanka, '"Yoü and I": Identity and the Performance of Self in Lady Gaga and Beyoncé', *Journal of Popular Culture*, vol. 49, no. 2 (2016), pp. 403-16

Kurth, Peter, *Isadora: A Sensational Life* (London 2003)

Lorde, Audre, *Sister Outsider: Essays and Speeches* (Berkeley 1984)

Mahon, Maureen, *Black Diamond Queens: African American Women and Rock and Roll* (Durham, NC, 2020)

Mangeshkar, Lata, and Nasreen Munni Kabir, *Lata Mangeshkar: In Her Own Voice* (New Delhi 2009)

Marcus, Sharon, *The Drama of Celebrity* (Princeton 2019)

Menon, Elizabeth K., *Evil by Design: The Creation and Marketing of the Femme Fatale* (Champaign, IL, 2006)

Moindrot, Isabelle, 'Mythologies of the Diva in Nineteenth Century French Theatre', in *Technology and the Diva: Sopranos, Opera, and Media from Romanticism to the Digital Age*, ed. Karen Henson (Cambridge 2016), pp. 24–36

Monroe, Marilyn, with Ben Hecht, *My Story* (New York 1974)

Negus, Keith, 'Cultural production and the corporation: musical genres and the strategic management of creativity in the US recording industry', *Media, Culture and Society*, vol. 20, no. 3 (1998), pp. 359–79

Nicholson, Stuart, *Ella Fitzgerald: A Biography of the First Lady of Jazz* (Boston, MA, 1995)

O'Brien, Lucy, *She Bop: The Definitive History of Women in Popular Music* (new edn London 2020)

Parish, James Robert, *Hollywood Divas* (Scotts Valley, CA, 2015)

Parton, Dolly, with Robert K. Oermann, *Dolly Parton, Songteller: My Life in Lyrics* (London 2020)

Ritz, David, *Respect: The Life of Aretha Franklin* (New York 2014)

Stephens, E.J., and Marc Wanamaker, *Early Warner Bros. Studios* (Mount Pleasant, SC, 2010)

Stine, Whitney, and Bette Davis, *Mother Goddam: The Story of the Career of Bette Davis* (Stroud 1974)

Stephen Tapert, *Best Actress: The History of Oscar-Winning Women* (New Brunswick 2019)

Tiffin, George, *A Star is Born: The Moment an Actress becomes an Icon* (London 2015)

Todd, Matthew, *Pride: The Story of the LGBTQ Equality Movement,* London 2019

Trier-Bienieck, Adrienne, ed., *The Beyoncé Effect: Essays on Sexuality, Race, and Feminism* (Jefferson, NC, 2016)

Vlastnik, Frank, and Laura Ross, *The Art of Bob Mackie* (New York 2021)

1   Moindrot 2016, p. 26.
2   Kerr 2015, pp. 102–4.
3   Anonymous sonnet dedicated to Carolina Passerini at Carnival Mantua, 1827, quoted in Cowgill and Poriss 2012, p. 8.
4   Ibid, p. 127.
5   Ibid., p. 124.
6   Ibid., p. 125.
7   Menon 2006, p. 143.
8   Limelight is the first form of spotlight used to intensely illuminate individual performers on stage. It was used from 1837 at the Covent Garden Theatre (later the Royal Opera House), London. Limelight is created when an oxyhydrogen flame is directed at a cylinder of quicklime (calcium oxide). In the first decade of the nineteenth century Humphry Davy showed that 'arclight' could also be cast by passing an electric current through a platinum strip. By the mid-nineteenth century arclight was being used to create visual effects such as sunlight or moonlight in order to reinforce the dramatic narratives and characters of grand opera. In 1887 the Paris Opera replaced gas lighting with electric lighting.
9   Cowgill and Poriss 2012, p. 23.
10  Etiquette for the Ladies: Eighty Maxims on Dress, Manners, and Accomplishments (London 1840), p. 28, quoted in Cowgill and Poriss 2012, p. 32.
11  'The Nouveau Flapper, www. sydneyflapper.wordpress.com/ 2018/10/07/morin-blossier-couturiers-to-the-courts-of-europe/ (accessed 22 June 2022).
12  The Los Angeles Times, 6 January 1912.
13  Ibid., 20 January 1907.
14  Cowgill and Poriss 2012, p. 176.
15  The Standard, 15 October 1919.
16  Cowgill and Poriss 2012, p. 179.
17  Kurth 2003, p. 149.
18  The Sphere, 10 October 1925, pp. 4–5
19  Kurth 2003, p. 150.
20  Quoted in 'Marie Lloyd and the music hall strike of 1907', www.unionancestors. co.uk (accessed 20 June 2022).

21  The 'Dance of the Seven Veils' originated with Oscar Wilde's play Salome. It was a description of the provocative dance that Salome performed for Herod Antipas in the New Testament to claim the severed head of John the Baptist.
22  Kurth 2003, p. 119.
23  Ibid.
24  Ibid.
25  Ibid., p. 529.
26  Alice Guy Blache (film director), quoted in Cochrane 2017, p. 9.
27  Jules-Rosette 2007, p. 47.
28  Baker created her banana skirt in 1926, and over the next decade transformed it from a basic design to a more abstract pattern. The skirt played an integral role in Baker's own choreography and through its evolving design reflects the changing character and agency of Baker herself. Jules-Rosette 2007, pp. 48–50.
29  Ibid., p. 214.
30  Trier-Bienieck 2016, p. 13.
31  'Sister Outsider, Transformation of Silence', in Lord 1984, p. 42.
32  'The Uses of Anger: Women Responding to Racism', in Lorde 1984, pp. 132–3.
33  Carman 2015, p. 32
34  'Bette Davis Vs. Warner Brothers', 13 July 2022, www.moviestvnetwork.com (accessed 20 August 2022).
35  Quoted in Life Magazine, 23 January 1939, p. 53.
36  Jenn Selby, 'International Women's Day; "When a man gives you his opinion..."', Independent online, www. independent.co.uk/news/people/news/ feminist-quotes-from-female-icons-to-inspire-you-on-international-women-s-day (accessed August 2022).
37  Daily Herald, 16 January 1936.
38  Los Angeles Times, 2 January 1947.
39  Mae West as Tira in I'm no Angel (1933).
40  Parish 2015, p. 270.
41  Kinematograph Weekly, 24 July 1952; Daily Mirror, 15 March 1952.
42  Interview with Marilyn Monroe, Life Magazine, 3 August 1962, p. 34.
43  Nicholson 2015, p. 149.
44  Life Magazine, 20 April 1959, p. 134.
45  Huffington 2002, p. 226.
46  Friedan 1963, p. 25.
47  Ibid., pp. 274–309.
48  Los Angeles Times, 19 March 1989.

49  John 2019, p. 101.
50  Callum Wells, 'Mariah Carey adds fuel to diva rumours...', Daily Mail Online, 3 December 2021.
51  Hadley Freeman, 'Mariah Carey: "They're calling me a diva? I think I'm going to cry!"', The G2 interview, Guardian, 5 October 2020.
52  ioneanalytics, 'Mariah Carey on being a Diva', TV One, 23 August 2017 (www. tvone.tv; accessed 16 August 2022).
53  Mickey Boardman, 'Mariah Carey Gets Revealing', Paper, www.papermag. com/mariah-carey-las-vegas-2474234371. html?rebelltitem=34#rebelltitem34 (accessed 2 September 2022).
54  www.latimes.com/entertainment-arts/ books/story/2022-02-10/in-defense-of-whitney-houston-author-gerrick-d-kennedy (accessed 12 September 2022).
55  '20 Lady Gaga Quotes That Will Make You Love Yourself More', Ultima Status, www.ultimastatus.com/20-lady-gaga-quotes-that-will-make-you-love-yourself-more/ (accessed 12 May 2022).
56  Trier-Bienieck 2016, p. 211.

**Shirley Bassey** in interview with Simon Hattenstone, *Guardian*, 24 October 2009, www.theguardian.com/music/2009/oct/24/shirley-bassey-interview

**Beyoncé** quoted in 'Claudia Rankine on How Beyoncé Became an Icon', *Harpers Bazaar*, 3 September 2021, www.harpersbazaar.com/culture/features/a37378121/claudia-rankine-beyonce-essay-september-2021/

**Maria Callas** quoted in her obituary by Raymond Ericson, *New York Times*, 17 September 1977

**Whitney Houston** in interview with Richard Corliss, *Time*, 11 July 1987

**Madonna** in interview at Cannes in 1991, for the promotion of her documentary *Truth or Dare*

**Lata Mangeshkar** in Mangeshkar and Munni Kabirl 2009

**Liza Minnell** in interview with Elisa Lipsky-Karasz, *Harpers Bazaar*, 18 February 2011, www.harpersbazaar.com/celebrity/latest/news/a673/liza-minnelli-interview/

**Marilyn Monroe** in *My Story,* with Ben Hecht (New York 1974)

**Elizabeth Taylor** interviewed by Johnny Carson on the Tonight Show, 21 February 1992, www.youtube.com/watch?v=1ZijnrYIMLk

**Rihanna** in interview with Mark Ellen, *Elle*, April 2013, www.elle.com/uk/fashion/celebrity-style/articles/a3165/rihanna-read-full-interview-elle-uk-april-2013/

1 Gloria Swanson as Norma Desmond in *Sunset Boulevard* (Paramount Pictures, 1950).
2 Glenn Close in *Sunset Boulevard: A Look Back* (Blu-ray special edition, 2000).
3 Gloria Anderson in ibid.
4 Stephens and Wanamaker 2010, p. 57.
5 'Bette Davis: A Basically Benevolent Volcano', *Arena* (BBC TV, 1983).
6 Ibid.
7 Ibid.
8 Bette Davis as Margo Channing in *All About Eve* (20th Century Fox, 1950).
9 'A Basically Benevolent Volcano' (note 5).
10 Ibid.
11 Ibid.
12 Stine and Davis 1974, p. 92.
13 Head and Calistro 1983, p. 110.
14 Joseph L. Mankiewicz in 'A Basically Benevolent Volcano' (note 5).
15 Ibid.
16 Stine and Davis 1974, p. 95.
17 Davis quoted in Ken Dickman, 'This is Bette Davis! How did you get my number?', *Advocate Magazine* (9 February 1977), pp. 30–1.
18 Stine and Davis 1974, p. 285.
19 Charles Busch, special features, *Bette and Joan: Duelling Divas, Whatever Happened to Baby* Jane (1963), (Blu-ray special edition, 2012).
20 Judy Garland, quoted in Tiffin 2015, p. 168.
21 Ibid.
22 Ibid., p. 59
23 'Seance at the Palace', *Time Magazine*, 18 August 1967.
24 Cited in Todd 2019, p. 34.
25 Dorothy's reply to this is: 'the queerness doesn't matter, so long as they're friends'.
26 Sylvia Rivera in *Stonewall Uprising* DVD (First Run Features 2010).
27 Liza Minnelli quoted in Tiffin 2015, p. 249.
28 Minnelli quoted in Tapert 2019, p. 88.
29 Cited in *Cleopatra: The Film That Changed Hollywood, Cleopatra* (1963) (Blu-ray Special Edition DVD 2001).
30 Ibid.
31 Cher quoted in Tapert 2019, p. 311.
32 Ibid.
33 Ibid.

34 Alex Needham, 'Review: Shirley Bassey', *Guardian* (2007), www.theguardian.com/music/2007/jun/24/glastonbury2007.glastonbury6 (accessed 15 September 2022)
35 A charitable organization established to help students, schools and communities reach their potential through music and performance.
36 Bob Mackie quoted in Vlastnik and Ross 2021, p. 169.

1    Highlander Folk School was founded
     in 1932 with the intention of providing
     a fully racially integrated location for '...
     the oppressed to gather, learn, organize,
     and make change'. The school's guests
     over the years included Dr Martin Luther
     King Jr, John Lewis and Rosa Parks. See
     www.americanswhotellthetruth.org/
     portraits/myles-horton/ (accessed 11 July
     2022).

2    Source: Library of Congress.

3    Du Bois 1903, p. 157.

4    NAACP, 'History of Lynching in America',
     www.naacp.org/find-resources/history-
     explained/history-lynching-america
     (accessed 11 July 2022).

5    The flag flew from 1920 to 1938. NAACP,
     'Our History', www.naacp.org/about/our-
     history (accessed 11 July 2022).

6    Holiday would later perform the song on
     BBC television in the 1950s.

7    The Mocambo Club's owner, Charlie
     Morrison, felt that Fitzgerald was not
     sufficiently 'glamorous' to attract an
     audience to the Hollywood nightclub.

8    Emmett Till, who was visiting relatives
     in Mississippi, was kidnapped, tortured
     and shot to death by two white men
     who believed the allegations of Carolyn
     Bryant (née Holloway) that he had
     'whistled' at and 'grabbed' her. Roy
     Bryant (her former husband) and his
     half-brother, J.W. Milam, were cleared of
     Till's murder in September 1955. They
     admitted to his killing in an interview
     with *Look* magazine in January 1956.

9    From an interview with Fred Robbins,
     who worked for New York's WHN
     radio. The interview was never aired,
     but parts of it were heard in the 2019
     documentary *Ella Fitzgerald: Just One of
     Those Things* (2019).

10   President Kennedy's live televised
     address to the nation on civil rights
     took place on 11 June 1963 (JFK Library,
     11 June, available at www.jfklibrary.
     org/learn/about-jfk/historic-speeches/
     televised-address-to-the-nation-on-
     civil-rights [accessed 12 July 2022]).
     The broadcast followed violent
     protests against the desegregation of
     the University of Alabama. During the

     broadcast Kennedy chastised those
     who opposed educational reform and
     integration while believing in American
     freedoms and opportunity for 'all'.

11   The March on Washington, during
     which Martin Luther King Jr delivered his
     'I Have a Dream' speech, was attended
     by an estimated crowd of more than
     250,000. See Official Program for the
     March on Washington (1963), www.
     archives.gov/milestone-documents/
     official-program-for-the-march-on-
     washington (accessed 11 July 2022).

12   The SNCC is the student chapter of the
     US civil rights movement, aligned to
     Martin Luther King Jr's SCLC.

13   'Aretha Says She'll Go Angela's Bond if
     Permitted,' *Jet Magazine* (December
     1970), p. 54.

14   Franklin performed at Carter's pre-
     inaugural celebration – the inaugural
     gala on 19 January 1977 – rather than at
     Carter's inauguration itself.

15   Hendrik Verwoerd was first Prime
     Minister of apartheid-ruled South Africa.

16   UN Audiovisual Library, '18th Meeting
     of Special Committee Against Apartheid'
     (16 July), www.unmultimedia.org/
     avlibrary/asset/2553/2553678/ (accessed
     11 July 2022).

17   The Pan Africanist Congress (PAC) was
     a South African political organization
     (later a political party) that advocated
     for Black South Africans.

18   Formerly the South African Native
     National Congress, the African National
     Congress (ANC) advocated for Black
     and Coloured voting rights and the end
     of apartheid, following its introduction
     in 1948.

19   Launched by CORE – Congress of Racial
     Equality – in 1961, Freedom Rides
     saw student activists ('Freedom
     Riders') travelling on buses that
     upheld segregation across state lines.
     Carmichael would later move away from
     the non-violence advocated by King
     and both organizations – favouring self-
     defence.

**RULE THE WORLD:**
STATUS, POWER, FREEDOM

1   'Rihanna Takes Flight', *Harper's Bazaar* (8 February 2017), www.harpersbazaar. com/culture/features/a20446/rihanna-amelia-earhart-photo-shoot/ (accessed 6 July 2022).

2   Parton 2020, p. 8.

3   O'Brien 2020, p. 150.

4   Barbara Walters interview, broadcast 1977, www.youtube.com/watch?v=If-oWqUYzIQ (accessed 3 July 2022).

5   When Colonel Tom Parker requested that Parton let Elvis record 'I Will Always Love You' (which would also mean handing over 50 per cent of the publishing rights to him), she refused. This was a difficult decision to make, as Dolly was a huge Elvis fan. Decades later she would go on to make millions of dollars following the release of Whitney Houston's version in 1992.

6   Charlie Rose interview, broadcast 2009, www.youtube.com/watch?v=i_mWY9ksLq4 (accessed 3 July 2022).

7   'Don't Rain on My Parade' has lived on as a standout moment in Streisand's oeuvre and has become a de facto gay anthem – joining others by (overwhelmingly female, overwhelmingly Black) performers such as Diana Ross's 'I'm Coming Out', 'I Will Survive' by Gloria Gaynor, 'Over the Rainbow' by Judy Garland and newly minted additions such as 'Born This Way' by Lady Gaga and 'Work Bitch' by Britney Spears in the pantheon of songs embraced by the LGBTQ+ community as queer songs of praise.

8   Gregg Kilday, 'Barbra Streisand on Hollywood's Double Standard: "What Does 'Difficult' Mean, Anyway?", *The Hollywood Reporter* (9 December 2015), www.hollywoodreporter.com/movies/movie-features/barbra-streisand-hollywoods-double-standard-845819/ (accessed 2 July 2022).

9   Khalid Mohamed, 'Marriage, Rivalry, Politics: Lata Mangeshkar Covers It All in Her Last Interview' (7 February 2022), www.thequint.com/entertainment/celebrities/lata-mangeshkar-last-extensive-interview-marriage-rivalry-politics#read-more (accessed 10 July 2022).

10  Hamish Bowles, 'Adele Had us Long Before "Hello"', *Vogue* (12 February 2016), www.vogue.com/article/adele-march-2016-cover (accessed 7 July 2022).

11  From 'The 30 Interview' with Zane Lowe, Apple Music (17 November 2021), www.youtube.com/watch?v=1gtPULpjzuA (accessed 2 July 2022).

12  Lisa Robinson, 'Above and Beyoncé', *Vanity Fair* (November 2005), www.archive.vanityfair.com/article/2005/11/above-and-Beyoncé (accessed 6 July 2022).

13  Beyoncé weathered a significant public backlash following her Black-power-aesthetic Superbowl performance in 2016. Some US police officers vowed to boycott her Formation World Tour as a punishment. Her response was to sell 'BOYCOTT BEYONCÉ' T-shirts as tour merchandise.

14  Reported in *NME*, 20 September 2012: www.nme.com/news/music/Beyoncé-247-1260446 (accessed 6 July 2022).

15  'Beyoncé in Her Own Words: Her Life, Her Body, Her Heritage', *Vogue* (6 August 2018), www.vogue.com/article/Beyoncé-september-issue-2018 (accessed 6 July 2022).

16  Lisa Robinson, 'Rihanna in Cuba', *Vanity Fair* (6 October 2015), www.vanityfair.com/hollywood/2015/10/rihanna-cover-cuba-annie-leibovitz (accessed 4 July 2022).

17  Ibid.

18  Megan Sauer, 'Rihanna is now worth $1.4 billion – making her America's youngest self-made billionaire woman', CNBC (4 July 2022), www.cnbc.com/2022/07/04/rihanna-is-now-americas-youngest-self-made-billionaire-woman.html (accessed 4 July 2022).

19  Afua Hirsch, 'Rihanna Talks New Music, Fenty Skincare and Her Plans To Have "3 Or 4 Kids"', *Vogue* (30 March 2020), www.vogue.co.uk/news/article/rihanna-new-album-vogue-interview (accessed 4 July 2022).

20  Robinson 2015 (note 16).

**EXPRESS YOURSELF:**
**REBEL REINVENTION**

1   Joe Lynch, 'Madonna Delivers Her Blunt Truth During Fiery, Teary Billboard Women In Music Speech', *Billboard* (9 December 2016), www.billboard.com/music/awards/madonna-billboard-woman-of-the-year-labrinth-7616927/ (accessed 3 June 2022).

2   Negus 1998, p. 377.

3   'Annenberg Inclusion Initiative's annual report on popular music reveals little progress for women', *USC Annenberg* (8 March 2021), www.annenberg.usc.edu/news/research-and-impact/annenberg-inclusion-initiatives-annual-report-popular-music-reveals-little (accessed 4 June 2022). Since 2018 this research centre at USC Annenberg has been doing valuable work monitoring the progress of women in all areas of the music industry. The figures show that women make up 21.6 per cent of all artists in the Billboard Hot 100 from 2012 to 2020. Hence divas need to be ever more inventive and creative to be noticed, promoted and recognized.

4   Braziel 2004, p. 12.

5   Braidotti 2015, p. 242.

6   O'Brien 2020, p. 92.

7   Ibid., p. 113.

8   Ibid., p. 110.

9   Burns and Lafrance 2002, p. 2.

10   Whitney Perry, 'Madonna Reveals Controversial NFT Project Featuring NSFW Content', *Glamour* (12 May 2022), www.glamour.com/story/madonna-controversial-nft-project-nsfw-content (accessed 28 May 2022).

11   'Lady Gaga: Inside The Outside' (25 April 2013), MTV, www.youtube.com/watch?v=Gjt-EW3Qguk (accessed 1 June 2022).

12   Kumari 2016, p. 404.

13   Candace McDuffie, 'What Lauryn Hill's Iconic "Miseducation" Album Means To Black Women', *Vibe* (20 August 2018), www.vibe.com/features/editorial/miseducation-of-lauryn-hill-black-women-importance-601266/ (accessed 28 May 2022).

14   Joan Morgan, 'They call me Ms Hill', *Essence* (16 December 2009), www.essence.com/news/they-call-me-ms-hill/ (accessed 7 December 2022).

15   Horsley 2020, p. 103.

16   Michelle Griffin, 'Young and pregnant: The summer of my buffalo stance', *Sydney Morning Herald* (1 January 2022), www.smh.com.au/lifestyle/life-and-relationships/young-and-pregnant-the-summer-of-my-buffalo-stance-20211223-p59jv6.html (accessed 30 May 2022).

17   O'Brien 2020, p. 256.

18   *Björk: The Inner or Deep Part of an Animal or Plant Structure*, DVD documentary directed by Ragnheidur Gestsdottir (One Little Indian, 2004).

19   Daisy Woodward, 'Meet the man behind Björk's out-of-this-world masks', *Dazed* (27 November 2017), www.dazeddigital.com/fashion/article/38197/1/meet-the-man-behind-bjorks-out-of-this-world-masks-james-merry-utopia (accessed 1 June 2022).

20   Ruth Saxelby, '"Art Angel", a FADER documentary about Grimes' (10 December 2015), www.thefader.com/2015/12/10/grimes-art-angel-documentary (accessed 2 June 2022).

21   Vanessa Willoughby, 'This Woman's Work: FKA Twigs's "MAGDALENE" Dissects Female Martyrdom, Bitchmedia (11 November 2019), www.bitchmedia.org/article/fka-twigs-magdalene-female-martyrdom-review (accessed 26 June 2022).

## NOTES

### I WANT TO BREAK FREE:
### LIBERATING THE DIVA

1   Carrie Brownstein, 'Fever Ray's Amazing
    Acceptance Speech, *NPR* (26 January
    2010), www.npr.org/sections/
    monitormix/2010/01/fever_rays_
    amazing_acceptance.html (accessed 28
    June 2022).
2   Marcus 2019, pp. 120–7.
3   Mahon 2020, p. 241; Kindle edn loc.
    5743.
4   Matthew Jacobs, 'Revisiting Tina Turner's
    Most Fabulous Looks', The Cut, *New York
    Magazine* (1 April 2021), www.thecut.
    com/2021/04/bob-mackie-revisits-tina-
    turner-looks.html (accessed 28 June
    2022).
5   'Gold & Platinum', *RIAA*, www.riaa.
    com/gold-platinum/?tab_active=default-
    award&se=tina+turner#search_section
    (accessed 28 June 2022).
6   Keith Cameron, 'Queen herald the age
    of the music video', *The Guardian* (11
    June 2011), www.theguardian.com/
    music/2011/jun/12/queen-herald-the-age
    (accessed 28 June 2022).
7   Jon Wilde, 'Queen: Killer Queen', *Uncut*
    (2005), *Rock's Backpages Library*,  www.
    rocksbackpages.com/Library/Article/
    queen-killer-queen (accessed 28 June
    2022).
8   'Live Aid- Queen- Full Set HQ',
    YouTube, uploaded by Astrolux777,
    8 March 2018, www.youtube.com/
    watch?v=TkFHYODzRTs&t=520s.

## NOTES

### ALL BY MYSELF:
### NEGOTIATING THE PUBLIC AND THE PRIVATE

1   Edith Piaf quoted in Pubali Dasgupta,
    'The light and dark of the legendary
    Edith Piaf, www.faroutmagazine.co.uk/
    rolling-stones-paint-it-black-story-brian-
    jones/ (accessed August 2022).
2   Sade interview for *Mercury News*,
    www.mercurynews.com/2011/08/04/
    sade-enjoying-life-on-the-road-again/
    (accessed September 2022).
3   Edith Piaf in www.youtube.com/
    watch?v=EVTDxMJjBP0 (at 10.13 mins).
4   See www.quoteikon.com/liza-minnelli-
    quotes.html (accessed August 2022).
5   Ibid.
6   Springfield interviewed in *Mojo*, July
    1995.
7   Sade quoted in Robert Sandall, 'Sade
    emerges from her country retreat', www.
    thetimes.co.uk/article/sade-emerges-
    from-her-country-retreat-h70c0x3v32r
    (accessed August 2022).
8   As did Curt Claudio in 1971, www.
    johnlennon.com/news/curt-claudio/
    (accessed August 2022).
9   Billie Eilish in Miranda Sawyer, 'Billie Eilish:
    "To always try to look good is such a loss
    of joy and freedom"', *Guardian* online,
    www.theguardian.com/music/2021/
    jul/31/billie-eilish-to-always-try-to-look-
    good-is-such-a-loss-of-joy-and-freedom
    (accessed August 2022).
10  Ibid.
11  Kevin Macdonald documentary, *Whitney*
    (2018).

# Author Biographies

**Kate Bailey** is Senior Curator and Producer, Theatre and Performance at the V&A. Her recent exhibitions include *Alice: Curiouser and Curiouser* (2021) and *Opera: Passion, Power and Politics* (2017).

**Veronica Castro** is the Exhibition Research Assistant for *Diva* and previously co-curated the *On Point: Royal Academy of Dance at 100* display at the V&A.

**Sasha Geffen** is author of *Glitter Up the Dark: How Pop Music Broke the Binary*, an analysis of queerness and gender nonconformity in the past century of popular music. Their writing has been published in *Artforum*, *The Nation*, *Rolling Stone*, *Pitchfork* and *Paris Review*, among others.

**Keith Lodwick** is a curator, film historian and writer. He was the Curator of Theatre and Screen Arts at the V&A.

**Lucy O'Brien** is an academic, writer and broadcaster. The 25th anniversary edition of her book *She Bop: The Definitive History of Women in Popular Music* was published in 2020. She is author of *Dusty: The Classic Biography* and *Madonna: Like An Icon*.

**Miranda Sawyer** is a writer, journalist and broadcaster, with a particular interest in Pop culture. Besides her features and audio criticism for the *Observer*, her writing has appeared in magazines such as *GQ* and *Vogue*. She is the author of *Park and Ride* and *Out of Time*.

**Jacqueline Springer** is V&A Curator, Africa and Diaspora: Performance. She specializes in the histories and sociologies of contemporary Black musics.

# Acknowledgements

We would like to thank the following people whose enthusiasm, dedication and vigour made the *Diva* exhibition and this book possible.

Our design team, who achieved so much with the space; Alicia Gonzalez-Lafita, Will Bindley, Jessica Hung Han Yun, Freya Spencer-Wood, Evonne Mackenzie and Boris Meister.

Our A/V team Tal Rosner, Nick Joyce and Rachael Shepherd, and our sound engineer Gareth Fry, all of whom brought such wonderful movement and life to the space, and enabled us to watch and hear our divas in action.

We are deeply indebted to colleagues from the V&A for their insight, knowledge and support. From the Exhibitions Department: Daniel Slater, Brendan Cormier, Zoe Louizos, Claire Everitt and Meg Hogg. From Loans: Belén Lasheras Díaz. From Interpretation: Asha McLoughlin, Lenny Cherry, Emilie Foyer and Bryony Shepherd. From Development: Stefanie Agar, Stacey Bowles and Imogen Nolan. Across the Collections and Research Departments: Christopher Wilk, Simon Sladen, Harriet Reed, Ellis, Niamh Kelly, Joanna Norman, Cathy Haill, Janet Birkett, Jane Pritchard, Oriole Cullen, Sonnet Stanfill, Jenny Lister, Zorian Clayton and Alice Power. In the Conservation Departments: Nigel Bamforth, Clair Battison, Katy Smith, Lara Flecker, Louisa Geddes, Marisa Kalvins, Eoin Kelly and Sarah Van Snick.

Thank you also to our Photographer, Sarah Duncan, and the brilliant work of the Technical Services team led by Richard Ashbridge.

To our brilliant authors, who have written about our divas so engagingly and sensitively: Sasha Geffen, Keith Lodwick, Lucy O'Brien, Miranda Sawyer and Jacqueline Springer. To our Publications team, whose tenacity and patience have made the process of writing and putting the book together an absolute pleasure: Coralie Hepburn, Rebecca Fortey, Lucy Macmillan, Andrew Tullis and Emma Woodiwiss. Also, to Joe Ewart for his fabulous book design.

To the institutions who have so generously agreed to lend us objects from their wonderful collections: Château des Milandes, Harewood House (Leeds), Hollywood Heritage Museum (Los Angeles) Musée Édith Piaf (Paris), National Museum of African American History and Culture (Smithsonian, Washington, DC), National Portrait Gallery (Smithsonian, Washington, DC) Natural History Museum of Los Angeles, Rock and Roll Hall of Fame (Cleveland), Royal Opera House (London), Smallhythe Place (Kent) and Sony Music UK.

To the following individuals, who have generously given their time and expertise: Richard Adkins, Gürsan Acar, Dylan Bailey, Alex Beard, Brian Becker, Derek Birkett, Thea Bragazzi, Jay Brown, Mona Card, Bex Cassie, Steven Ciccone, Dolce Cioffo, David Corio, Greer Crawley, Julia Creed, Roger Davies, Edwina Dunn, Emily Eavis, Alan Edwards, Pam and Jim Elyea, Nicola Formichetti, Lisa Garrett, Cassandra Gracey, Jenelle Hamilton, Tobias Heinrichs, Philipp Hinz, Steve Hodges, Pam Hogg, Dorothy Hui, Craig Inciardi, Joanna Kalli, Charlotte Knight, Nick Knight, Angélique de Labarre de Saint-Exupéry, Deborah Landis, Duran Lantink, Joe McFate, Bob Mackie, Mitch Maguire, Thomas Manzi, Oliver Mears, Jenny Kern Meredith, James Merry, Vicki Mortimer, Jen O'Hill, Nwaka Onwusa, Denis O'Regan, Naomi Parry, Tara Peterson, Sandy Powell, Dwandalyn Reece, Christian Reiche, Sheila Rock, Auriane Roulland, Jule Rubi, Chris Salmon, Angie Schneider, Greg Schreiner, Anne Sebba, John Shearlaw, Justin Thornton, Norman Tipton, Alex Tutuianu, Kathryn Uhde, Iris Van Herpen, Viktor & Rolf, Beth Werling and the team at Vivienne Westwood.

Finally, an enormous thank you to the divas featured in our exhibition, who continue to entertain and inspire us: Adele, Arca, Joan Baez, Dame Shirley Bassey, Beyoncé, Björk, Mariah Carey, Cher, Priyanka Chopra, Danielle de Niese, Joyce DiDonato, Doja Cat, Billie Eilish, Missy Elliott, Fairuz, Debbie Harry, PJ Harvey, Lauryn Hill, Janet Jackson, Sir Elton John, Grace Jones, Lady Gaga, Deborah Landis, Annie Lennox, Lil Nas X, Lizzo, Madonna, Bette Midler, Liza Minnelli, Janelle Monáe, Dolly Parton, P!nk, Leontyne Price, Rihanna, Diana Ross, Sade, Siouxsie Sioux, Patti Smith, Britney Spears, Barbra Streisand, Tina Turner, and those who are no longer with us.

*Kate Bailey, Veronica Castro*
*Exhibition curators*

# Image Credits

© 2022 The Andy Warhol Foundation for the Visual Arts, Inc./Licensed by DACS, London: p. 2

Photo: Kevin Mazur/MG18/Getty Images for The Met Museum/Vogue: p. 5

Photo: © Viðar Logi: p. 6

Photograph © David Corio: p. 10

Photo: © Angus McBean. © Harvard Theatre Collection, Houghton Library, Harvard University: p. 11

Reproduced courtesy of Harewood House Trust: p. 12

Mary Evans Picture Library: p. 24

Photo: Apic/Getty Images: p. 28

Permission granted by Ministero della cultura – Pinacoteca di Brera – Biblioteca Braidense, Milano: p. 31

© ADAGP, Paris and DACS, London 2022: p. 32

Photo: ScreenProd/Photononstop/Alamy Stock Photo: p. 34

Margaret Herrick Library, Academy of Motion Picture Arts and Sciences: p. 35

Photo: Collection Christophel/Alamy Stock Photo/courtesy Columbia Pictures p. 36

Courtesy 20th Century Fox: p. 37

Photo: Silver Screen Collection/Getty Images: p. 38

Photo: Herbert Dorfman/Corbis via Getty Images: p. 39

© Estate of Alan Fletcher: p. 40

Photo: Bettmann/Getty Images: p. 41

Photo: Michael Ochs Archives/Getty Images: p. 43

Photo: Louis Mélançon/copyright Metropolitan Opera: p. 45

Photo: Houston Rogers/© Victoria and Albert Museum, London: p. 46

© Estate of Alan Barlow: p. 47

Photo: © Keystone Press Agency/Keystone USA via ZUMAPRESS.com/Alamy Stock Photo: p. 48

Photo: Josh Brasted/FilmMagic/Getty Images: p. 50

Photo: Rogan Ward Ward. REUTERS/Alamy Stock Photo: p. 52

Courtesy RCA Records: p. 53 (above)

Courtesy Voix De L'Orient: p. 53 (below)

Photo: Denis O'Regan: p. 56

Photograph © David Corio: p. 57

Photo: Gotham/GC Images/Getty Images: p. 58

Photo: Kevin Mazur/WireImage/Getty Images: 59

Photo: © Victoria and Albert Museum, London: pp. 60-1

Photo: Harry Hammond/© Victoria and Albert Museum, London: p. 62

Courtesy Paramount Pictures Corporation: p. 64

20th Century Fox/Photofest: p. 66

The New York Public Library/Art Resource, NY: p. 68

Photo: Bettmann/Getty Images: p. 70

Photo: Bettmann/Getty Images: p. 71

Original Artwork by Costume and Fashion Designer, Bob Mackie: p. 74

Photo: Edd Westmacott/Alamy Stock Photo: p. 75

Photo: Frank Carroll/NBCU Photo Bank/Getty Images: p. 76

Original Artwork by Costume and Fashion Designer, Bob Mackie: p. 77

Photo: Ron Davis/Getty Images: p. 78

Courtesy World Of Wonder Productions: p. 79

Photo: Mark Sullivan/Contour by Getty Images: p. 80

Original Artwork by Costume and Fashion Designer, Bob Mackie: p. 81

Photo: Hulton Archive/Getty Images: p. 82

Photo: Harry Hammond/© Victoria and Albert Museum, London: p. 84

Photo: Charles Peterson/Hulton Archive/Getty Images: p. 86

Photo: Harry Hammond/© Victoria and Albert Museum, London: pp. 88-9

Ella Fitzgerald Papers, Archives Center, National Museum of American History, Smithsonian Institution: p. 91

Photo: Bettmann/Getty Images: p. 92

Collection of the Smithsonian National Museum of African American History and Culture, Gift from the Trumpauer-Mulholland Collection: p. 94 (above)

Collection of the Smithsonian National Museum of African American History and Culture: p. 94 (below)

Photograph © David Corio: p. 95

Photo: David Redfern/Redferns/Getty Images: p. 96

Collection of the Smithsonian National Museum of African American History and Culture: p. 97

Bentley Historical Library, University of Michigan. C. L. Franklin Papers 1957-1991, 1963-1984. Volume/Box: Box 1: p. 98

Photo: Ron Edmonds/AP/Shutterstock: p. 99

Poster: Scott Meola, Simplissimus, courtesy Milestone Films: p. 101

UN Photo/Teddy Chen: p. 102

Photo: Craig McDean/Art + Commerce/ (courtesy Hope Powell Estate): p. 104

Photo: The Dollywood Company: p. 106

Photo: Silver Screen Collection/Getty Images: p. 108

Photo: PictureLux/The Hollywood Archive Alamy Stock Photo/courtesy MGM/UA Entertainment/Ladbroke Entertainments Ltd: p. 110

Photo: STRDEL/Stringer/AFP via Getty Images: p. 111

Photo: UPI Photo/Phil McCarten/Alamy Stock Photo: p. 112

Photo: Eugene Adebari/Shutterstock: p. 114

Courtesy Parkwood Entertainment LLC: p. 116

Photo: Larry Busacca/Getty Images for Coachella: p. 117

Photo: Kevin Mazur/Getty Images for Fenty Beauty by Rihanna: p. 119

Photo: RANDY BROOKS/AFP/Getty Images: p. 120

Photo: Sergione Infuso /Corbis via Getty Images: p. 121

Photograph © David Corio: p. 122

© 1969=davidedwardbyrd=2022: p. 125

© Estate of Brian Maloney: p. 126

© Robert Mapplethorpe Foundation. Used by permission: p. 127

© Chris Stein | Rednight, Inc.: p. 129

Sheila Rock Photography: p. 130

Photo: Rob Verhorst/Redferns/Getty Images: p. 131

Photo: Dimitrios Kambouris/Getty Images: p. 132

Photo: Michael Campanella/Getty Images: p. 133

Courtesy Columbia Records/Sony Music: p. 134

Courtesy Interscope Records: p. 135

Photo: Kevin Mazur/Getty Images: p. 136

Photo: Kevin Mazur/Getty Images: p. 137

Photo: © Jean Baptiste Mondino: p. 138

Courtesy The Goldmind Inc.: p. 140-1

Photo: Santiago Felipe: p. 142

Photo: Rodolfo Sassano/Alamy Stock Photo: p. 144

Photo: Tabatha Fireman/Female Perspective/ Alamy Live News: p. 145

Photograph © David Corio: p. 146

# Index

189

I never took the easy path, always the rough one. But when I took it, I wanted to make it easier for those who followed me.

Joséphine Baker